Truman's GRANDVIEW FARM

JON TAYLOR

Charleston  London

THE
History
PRESS

Published by The History Press
Charleston, SC 29403
www.historypress.net

Cover images courtesy of the Truman Library and the author.

First published 2011

Manufactured in the United States

ISBN 978.1.60949.089.8

Library of Congress Cataloging-in-Publication Data

Taylor, Jon.
Truman's Grandview farm / Jon Taylor.
p. cm.
Includes bibliographical references and index.
ISBN 978-1-60949-089-8
1. Truman, Harry S., 1884-1972--Homes and haunts--Missouri--Grandview. 2. Truman,
Harry S., 1884-1972--Childhood and youth. 3. Truman, Harry S., 1884-1972--Family.
4. Farm life--Missouri--Grandview. 5. Grandview (Mo.)--History. 6. Presidents--United
States--Biography. I. Title.
E814.T39 2011
973.918092--dc22
[B]
2011009603

CONTENTS

Introduction   5

1. A City Boy Returns to His Roots   11
2. Anatomy of a Six-Hundred-Acre Farm   23
3. J.A. Truman & Son, Farmers   34
4. Pursuits Off the Farm   56
5. The Courtship   72
6. Harry Truman: Political Farmer   96
7. The Farm from 1917 to 1995   109

Notes   117
Index   125
About the Author   127

INTRODUCTION

On September 12, 1957, Harry Truman unveiled a plaque in Grandview, Missouri, at the newly constructed Truman Corners Shopping Center. The Truman family had sold a portion of their family farm to the Don Casto Corporation, which then oversaw the construction of the shopping center that came to be known as Truman Corners. In a short speech delivered at the dedication, Truman talked about his farming career, which had started in 1906 and had come to a close in 1917, when he enlisted to serve in World War I. Truman's attendance at the dedication was quite remarkable because it allowed him to reflect on the significant changes he had witnessed throughout his life. Not only was he able, by 1957, to see the impact of mechanized farming, but he also saw the impact of urbanization. He was a firm believer in progress, as evidenced by the inscription written on the plaque:

> *Two boys, Harry S. Truman and J. Vivian Truman once lived on, worked and ploughed the farmland on which this shopping center now stands. In the great American tradition one boy went from these fields to become the President of the United States. The brother and sister became outstanding civic leaders.*
>
> *Now, in one lifetime the farm again contributes to the great American dream of opportunity and progress by becoming the site of one of the nation's finest shopping centers—Truman Corners Town and Country Shoppers City, dedicated to the Truman family, the people of Greater Kansas City and all the United States—this could happen only in America.*

However, in his speech, he noted that he would have preferred to keep the farm in the family, but "we know progress pays no attention to the individual."[1] Truman's belief in progress was born out of his personality and the experiences he had on the farm, as well as his ability to look back on his farming days and make comparisons with what farming had become by 1957. To Truman, it was like night and day—farming had literally moved from relying on animal and human power to being transformed by machine.[2] He realized this in the hard-fought 1948 election campaign. Speaking in Dexter, Iowa, he said:

> *Now you can get on a tractor and plow night and day—you don't have to feed it or water it—you can get off it whenever you please, take a nap, come back and run it again. I didn't live on the farm in this age. I'm sorry I didn't. I don't want to turn the clock back. I don't want to go back to the horse and buggy age.*[3]

Historians have debated what Harry Truman's farming experience meant. Stephen Slaughter, son of Orlando Vinton Slaughter, Truman neighbor and Slaughter family historian, believed that Harry Truman's farming experience represented the American frontier. He wrote:

> *It was not the frontier of Andrew Jackson, or William Henry Harrison, or of Abraham Lincoln; there were few log cabins in Missouri, almost none in Jackson County, but these people came out of Tennessee and Kentucky in the 1830s, the 1840s, and the 1850s, they set up a new life in a new state, and from the state settlers went out to the Northwest, to Oregon and Washington, and to the Southwest.*

Slaughter continued, "These were Harry Truman's people and in that sense he represented the end of an era, the last occupant of the White House with a genuine flavor of the frontier in his upbringing and in his blood."[4]

Richard Kirkendall was one of the first to weigh in on the significance of the time Truman spent on the farm. He argued that for Truman, it was "a period of personality change in which [he] became less withdrawn, much more gregarious, much more sociable and popular, much more confident in his relations with other people than he had been in earlier years."[5] Kirkendall wrote his article prior to the release of over two hundred letters that Harry Truman sent to Bess while he was on the farm, and noted Truman scholar Robert Ferrell used these letters to draft the first book on Truman's farming experiences. In this book, he argued that Truman's experience on the farm allowed him to take three things with him to the White House. First, Ferrell agreed with Truman's mother, who said that it "was on the farm that Harry got all his common sense. He didn't get it in town."[6] Second, Truman took the ability to work hard. Ferrell wrote, "Observers noticed how he [as president] could turn out paperwork, efficiently and without any feeling that afterward he had to rest."[7] Third, Ferrell argued that it was on the farm that Truman developed a "desire to see people." Ferrell concluded, "All these qualities—common sense, ability to work, liking people—served the nation during the perilous time when Truman was president."[8]

In the 1990s, three authors produced biographies that covered Truman's farming experience, and each biographer interpreted the farm years in slightly different ways. David McCullough's biography appeared in 1992, and he essentially agreed with Robert Ferrell's interpretation about the significance of the farm years when he wrote, "He [Truman] never lost the farm habits of early rising and hard work. His mother would say the farm was where Harry got his common sense."[9] Robert Ferrell published a biography in 1994, and in this biography he explored in greater detail the significance of Harry Truman's farming career than he had in his 1991 book. He argued that Truman learned from his farming experiences a "kind of formula that he applied to politics. The formula was that hard work plus patience would amount to the best he could do, after which he had to let nature take its course." Furthermore, Ferrell said that Truman learned the trait of "stoicism" from his experiences, and a third characteristic that he took away with him was the importance of solitude. Connected with solitude was the idea that Truman's farming experiences "afforded [him] the perspective needed to dream of bigger things." Ferrell pushed his conclusion further and argued that it was through the challenges and struggles that Truman went through on the farm that he discovered that he was "good enough, able enough, to undertake larger tasks if they somehow, in some yet unknown way, presented themselves."[10] Alonzo Hamby rounded out the Truman biographies when he published *A Life of Harry S. Truman: Man of the People* in 1995, and his analysis went beyond the perceived personality traits that the other historians argued Truman acquired as a result of his farming experiences. Hamby noted that the "extended family with which Harry lived for some ten years molded his character and personality as much as any other source," but then, unlike the other historians, Hamby also noted that Truman's farming experience was not all positive when he concluded that "years of work with little material gain [on the farm] sapped him psychologically."[11]

INTRODUCTION

The most recent work on the Truman farm is *Farm Roots and Family Ties*, written by Gail E.H. Evans-Hatch and D. Michael Evans-Hatch for the National Park Service. In this book-length treatment of Truman's farm career, the authors asked how his farming experiences influenced his political career. They concluded that his status as a farmer was not the most influential factor in explaining the political support he received as a senator, vice president and president. They believed that Truman's farming status was but one factor that voters examined. They argued that his farming status must be coupled with his role in the Masons and in veterans groups as other ways voters came to identify and support Harry Truman; however, the authors did not examine in any great detail the speeches Truman delivered on the campaign trail when he ran for Eastern Jackson County judge, presiding judge, senator, vice president or president. While it is true that Harry Truman appealed to various constituencies in 1948, it was certainly clear that at no other time and in no other election was he as frank with the voters about his farming experiences than he was in that close election. Capturing the farm vote was clearly on his radar screen in 1948, but it is still harder to tell if voters in some of the farm states that went for Truman supported him because he had been a farmer or because they were the beneficiaries of help under the Democratic New Deal agricultural programs.[12]

However, I am not sure voters in 1948 cared whether Harry Truman was a Mason or whether he had any military experience. It would stand to reason that Truman's status as a farmer, Mason and World War I vet would have been more important to voters in his early local and state elections than in the national election in 1948. Still, in 1948 he talked more about farming than he had in any of his previous campaigns. Clearly the farm vote was important to him, and apparently some of his campaigning did pay off.

Truman's experience as a farmer did have an impact on his later political career because it allowed him to identify with many Missourians who also were farmers when he ran for Eastern Jackson County judge, U.S. senator, vice president in 1944 and president in 1948. While he was on the farm, Truman became involved in the Masons and served in the Missouri National Guard. These experiences would pay dividends to him later in life. I have always regarded Truman as a "builder"—someone who took his experiences and continued to build on them throughout his life. While most scholars have argued that Truman's seminal life experience began with his service in World War I, I argue that Truman's experience on the farm was one of the key building blocks of his political career. It is true that Truman might not have entered politics if he had not had military experience; however, if he had not been able to couple that experience with the fact that he was a Jackson County farmer, I do not believe he would have experienced as much political success as he did. Furthermore, besides former president Jimmy Carter, Harry Truman was really the only other twentieth-century president who can claim the occupation of farmer.

The purpose of this book is to explain where Truman farmed, the people he worked with, the type of farm he operated and what pursuits he was involved in while he was on the farm. It was on the farm that he began a nine-year courtship with one of his former Independence High School classmates, Bess Wallace. Their relationship will be examined through the many letters the couple exchanged from 1910 to 1917. Furthermore, this book will try to assess the significance of Truman's farming experience within the scholarly context outlined above. It will conclude by briefly describing how the farm came to be preserved and operated by the National Park Service.

A City Boy Returns
to His Roots

In 1906, Harry Truman, at the age of twenty-two, heeded the call of his family and came to work a six-hundred-acre farm located near Grandview, Missouri. He had been working at a bank in downtown Kansas City. The farm was owned by his maternal grandmother, Harriett Louisa Gregg Young, who first came to Jackson County in 1841 from Shelby County, Kentucky, with her husband, Solomon Young. The Youngs, who were married on January 9, 1838, in Kentucky, were Jackson County pioneers. Solomon Young purchased a significant amount of land in Jackson County and became a prominent individual there. While Solomon Young was a significant landholder, he served as one of the county's unofficial loan officers. In a time and place where there were few banks present, Young frequently held land as collateral for loans he extended to others who came to settle in the area. As the county continued to grow, he also recognized an opportunity to engage in America's westward expansion when he began freighting goods to those who traveled into the West. It has been documented that between 1846 and 1857, Young transported goods into the West that were sold either to settlers or to the United States government and delivered to various western forts. When the nation's westward expansion cooled and the railroads replaced the freighters, Solomon Young focused on raising grain-fed cattle on his vast Missouri landholdings.

In 1867, Solomon and Harriet Young purchased 398 acres of land just north of present-day Grandview, Missouri, bringing their total holdings to almost 2,000 acres. The couple constructed an imposing home (not the present-day farmhouse) on the property. The two-story home, built in the Colonial style, was forty-three feet wide and included a cellar and a central

Solomon Young, Harry Truman's maternal grandfather. *Truman Library*.

Harriet Young, Harry Truman's maternal grandmother. *Truman Library*.

fireplace. In fact, Mary Ethel Noland, one of Harry Truman's cousins, only remembered "the big parlor where the piano was and this gallery or veranda, a long veranda, on the side of the house where we played as children." She described the house as large, impressive and "very comfortable and roomy, because Solomon Young had a big family of daughters and two sons; one of them, Harrison Young."[13]

Solomon Young, along with his daughter, Martha Ellen, planted a grove of maple trees in front of the home in the fall of 1868. The main entrance to the farm was some two hundred yards away from the home, and also by the entrance where the Blue Ridge Baptist Church, which had been there since 1848, had its corresponding cemetery. Today, the church is no longer present, but the cemetery remains.

Harry Truman's grandmother, Harriet Young, was not to be underestimated. In this pioneer environment of Jackson County, while Solomon was freighting goods along the trails, she managed not only the household affairs but also the financial affairs of the family. Her name appears frequently on the deeds and other financial documents that attest to her status. There was no guarantee that Solomon

Young would return from these freighting trips, and in one instance he was gone for three years. Legally, the Youngs did what they could to protect their financial interests.

During the Civil War, the farm was a frequent target for Union troops, even though Solomon Young signed a loyalty oath on July 15, 1862. Between 1861 and 1864, Union forces took mules, hogs and other foodstuffs from the Youngs. Years later, Young unsuccessfully sued the federal government for the losses the family incurred during the war.

After the Civil War, Anderson Shipp Truman and his wife, Mary Jane Holmes Truman, who had come into Missouri in the fall of 1846 from Shelby County, Kentucky, moved near the Solomon Young farm. Prior to the move, the couple had lived on several farms in Jackson and Platte Counties before returning to Jackson County after the war. The farm they settled probably included a couple hundred acres that were valued at $9,000, which included the value of their real and personal property.

Anderson Shipp Truman and Mary Jane (Holmes) Truman had five children, including John A. Truman, who was born on December 5, 1851, in Jackson County. By 1880, John A. Truman was listed as a farmer, alongside his father, and the census revealed that the father and son were responsible for 180 acres of land, of which they had 60 acres planted in Indian corn, 10 acres in oats and 30 acres wheat. It appeared that the majority of their cereals went to feed forty head of swine, and they valued their farming operation, which included the land, implements and livestock, at $5,650. Mary Jane (Holmes) Truman died on February 15, 1879.[14]

Anderson Shipp Truman, Harry Truman's paternal grandfather. *Truman Library.*

The Truman farm was located one section over from the Young farm, and since both families were of the Baptist faith and the closest church was the Blue Ridge Baptist Church, located near the Young farm, this is probably where John A. Truman met one of Solomon and Harriet's daughters, Martha Ellen Young. John A. Truman's father served as a deacon in the church, and Harriet had joined the church in 1872. It is unclear whether John A. Truman actually joined the church, but he married Martha Ellen Young at Solomon and Harriet's farmstead on December 28, 1881. The couple did not stay in the area but moved ninety miles to the south, to Lamar, Missouri, where John A. Truman established himself as a livestock trader. John A. Truman's father, Anderson Shipp Truman, joined the newlyweds in Lamar.[15]

In Lamar, the couple had their first son. Harry Truman was born on May 8, 1884; however, their time in Lamar was short-lived. The family left in 1885 and returned to Harrisonville, Missouri, where they lived briefly on a farm. In 1886, they moved to a farm southeast of Belton, where John Vivian Truman was born on April 25, 1886.

In 1887, Solomon Young called the Truman family to work the Young farm in Grandview. Anderson Truman, who was still living with the Truman family, also moved to the Young farm. Having two grandfathers under one roof was quite a treat for two grandsons. Of the farming partnership formed between John Truman and Solomon Young, Harry Truman remembered:

John A. Truman and Martha Ellen (Young) Truman, Harry Truman's parents. *Truman Library*.

J. A. TRUMAN,
FEED AND SALE STABLES.

White Barn, Main Street, Near Mo. P. Depot,

LAMAR, MISSOURI.

MULES AND HORSES BOUGHT AND SOLD.

Above: *Papers of Mary Jane Truman, Truman Library.*

Right: Harry and Vivian Truman, circa 1890. *Truman Library.*

He and Grandpa Young were partners in the operation of the farm and the handling of herds of cattle and mules as well as hogs and sheep. I became familiar with every sort of animal on the farm and watched the wheat harvest, the threshing and the corn shucking, mowing and stacking hay, and every evening at suppertime heard my father tell a dozen farm hands what to do and how to do it. In addition to the six hundred acres where we lived, there was another farm of nine hundred or a thousand acres four miles away, which had to be operated too.[16]

Unfortunately, Grandpa Truman died on July 3, 1887. Harry Truman remembered that his funeral was held at the Young farm and that all three of his daughters were present. It was apparently Truman's first remembrance of the Young farm. He went on to recall, "I was four years old and was very curious about what was happening. Grandpa Truman was a grand man and petted me a great deal. He was a strong Baptist and violently anti-Catholic."[17]

However, not all of Truman's memories of the farm were like his first memory. He remembered the fun times that he had playing with Vivian:

My brother Vivian was two years my junior and he had lovely long curls. Grandpa [Young] and I cut off his curls one day by putting him in a highchair out on the south porch. Mamma was angry enough to spank us both, but she had such respect for her father that she only frowned at him. One day after the hair-cutting episode I sat on the edge of a chair in front of the mirror to comb my hair—I fell off the chair backwards and broke my collarbone—my first but not my last broken bone. Later in this same room I was eating a peach and swallowed the seed. Almost choked to death but mamma pushed the seed down my throat with her finger and I lived to tell about it.

Vivian and I used to play in the south pasture—a beautiful meadow in bluegrass. At the end of the grove was a mudhole. This grove was row on row of beautiful maple trees, a quarter of a mile long and six rows wide. We had a little red wagon which we took with us on our adventures in the pasture. We finally wound up at the mudhole with a neighbor boy about our age and I loaded Vivian and John Chancellor into the little wagon, hauled them into the mudhole—and upset the wagon. What a spanking I received. I can feel it yet! Every stitch of clothes on all three of us had to be changed, scrubbed, and dried, and so did we![18]

Truman also remembered the birth of his sister Mary Jane, named after her paternal grandmother, at the Young farm on August 12, 1889. Truman recalled, "We heard her cry upstairs and thought we had a new pet until our father told us we had a new sister."[19] Apparently, Mary Jane Truman did not hold this against her brother because she later fondly recalled the relationship she had with both her brothers:

> *Yes, he rocked me to sleep. He'd rock me to sleep till I was four or five years old. I can remember. We had a big old willow chair. It was big enough for him and me both to sit in the seat, and he'd put a pillow behind me and rock and rock and rock and sing "Bye Baby Bye." Mamma said I'd just get to sleep, and he'd try to stick his arm out and I'd bob up and he'd have to go through the whole process again. Then she said that he'd go out and play and then he'd get to thinking I couldn't breathe, so he'd come back in and check on me to see if I was breathing.*
>
> *It's funny how you're cute when you're kids. But he and Vivian were awful good to take me places and play with me and take me anywhere I needed to go.*[20]

Mary Jane Truman, circa 1890. *Truman Library*.

17

In 1892, tragedy struck the Young farm when Solomon Young died. At the time of his death, his estate was valued at $5,616.80. The probate inventory listed sixty tons of hay, 749 bushels of corn, 545 bushels of wheat in the barn and seventy-eight steers, which points to the fact that the farm was participating in the grain-fed agricultural industry prevalent in western Missouri after the end of the Civil War.[21]

Another tragedy struck the Young farm in 1894. The house that Harriet and Solomon constructed after the war burned to the ground. The *Belton Herald* reported:

> *The burning of the old Sol Young homestead on Wednesday evening, this past week, was a regrettable occurrence to the whole community. The fire was caused by a Negro girl, who, while filling a lamp spilled some coal oil on the floor, and when she lighted the lamp, she dropped the burning match in the puddle of oil and the flames were instantly beyond control. Harrison Young was at home, and so was his sister Mrs. John Bartleson and her two daughters, also Mrs. Sol Young. Nothing was saved from the fire but some bedding. The accumulation of years was swept away. There was no insurance on the house. The house will probably be rebuilt.*[22]

Harriet and her son, Harrison, quickly worked on a replacement structure that eventually came to be the current farm home.

When Harry Truman moved to the farm in 1906, there were some marked changes. The place was crowded. He found his younger brother, Vivian, there, along with his sister Mary Jane and his mother and father, Martha Ellen and John A. Truman. His grandmother, Harriet, and her brother, Harrison Young, as well as some hired hands, rounded out the crowded home constructed after the 1894 fire.

Besides being crowded, the farm was considerably smaller than the one his grandfather Solomon would have known. By 1906, the acreage of the farm had shrunk from a couple thousand acres to a mere 600 acres. However, when the 600-acre farm was compared with the average size of a Missouri farm around the turn of the century—about 125 acres—it was a significant operation.[23]

Truman's parents were remarkable. His mother, Martha Ellen, had encouraged all her children to attend public schools, and in 1890 the family moved from a farm to Independence, Missouri, so all three children could attend the Independence Public School system. According to Truman, his mother was the disciplinarian in the family:

A City Boy Returns to His Roots

We were taught that punishment always followed transgression and my mother saw to it that it did. She kept a good switch and a slipper handy for application to the spot where most good could be accomplished on young anatomy. My father never did punish me except an occasional scolding, which hurt worse than a good spanking would have.[24]

In contrast to his mother, historians have portrayed Truman's father as the risk taker in the family because he liked to gamble on ventures that always seemed to end up on the negative side of the balance sheet. It is true that John A. Truman's bet on Kansas City grain futures probably cost his eldest son an opportunity to go to college, but he was known as an excellent judge of livestock. However, if one closely examines the people in Truman's family, he will quickly conclude that John was not the only risk taker. Solomon Young's freighting business was also a very risky venture, so John A. Truman's ventures should not be viewed as something out of the ordinary.

Truman remembered his father in the following manner:

My father was a very honorable man. If he guaranteed a horse in a horse trade that guarantee was as good as a bond. If he agreed to do a day's work for a certain amount of money he'd give good measure on the work. He always expected the people who worked for him to give him a day's work for a day's pay—and woe to a loafer. He made the poll tax workers work for the county just as they worked for themselves…I was taught that the expenditure of public money is a public trust and I have never changed my opinion on that subject.[25]

Harry enjoyed being back with family, even if they were in uncomfortable proximity to one another. Of his grandmother and father, he wrote:

My grandmother was eighty-eight years old at the time [in 1906, when Harry Truman came back to the farm] *but as hale and hearty as a woman of fifty. She was a grand old lady. Had helped make my grandfather a successful man. She was a good Baptist, a strong sympathizer with the Confederate States of America and an Indian fighter on her own. She has told me a great many stories of conditions in Jackson County in the 1840s. My grandfather ran a wagon train from Westport and Independence to Salt Lake City and San Francisco from 1844 to the late sixties and my grandmother kept the five thousand-acre Jackson County farms going. She not only raised her own children—seven of them to be grown—two died as*

Mary Jane Truman,
Harrison Young and
Harriet Young (seated),
circa 1900. *Truman Library*.

*children—but she raised a couple of nephews and numerous slave children
and neighbor orphans. She had the most beautiful red hair I've ever seen,
and a kindly, benevolent attitude to those she liked.*[26]

Truman was also fond of his uncle Harrison:

*I was named for…Harrison Young. I was given the diminutive Harry
and, so that I could have two initials in my given name, the letter S was
added. My Grandfather Truman's name was Anderson Shipp Truman and
my Grandfather Young's name was Solomon Young, so I received the S for
both of them.*

*I was very fond of my Uncle Harrison. He was a big man a little
over six feet in height and he weighed 201 pounds. He was as strong as a
wrestler and was very good looking.*

*He remained a bachelor all his life and was a good story teller. He was
also a genius at games of chance, checkers, chess, poker, pitch, cooncan,
and sevenup.*

*He lived on the farm with my Grandmother Young, raised fine cattle,
hogs and sheep. It was my custom and brother's also to spend a lot of time
on the old home farm with Uncle Harrison and our Grandmother.*[27]

A City Boy Returns to His Roots

Above: Mary Jane
Truman on the farm.
Truman Library.

Right: John Vivian
Truman on the
farm, circa 1906–11.
Truman Library.

Harry Truman on the farm. *Truman Library.*

The farm did not remain crowded for long. In 1909, Grandma Young died, and Truman's father, John A. Truman, passed away in 1914. Harrison Young died in 1916, leaving Harry, Mary Jane and Martha Ellen Truman to manage the farm. Harry's brother, Vivian, married in 1911 and moved out to manage his own farm. Harry left the farm in 1917 to serve in World War I, and Vivian returned to the farm in 1930 to build his own home just to the north of the 1894 home. He and his sons farmed the area until the 1950s. Harry Truman never returned to the farm to live after he married Bess Wallace in 1919; instead, he came only for family visits.

ANATOMY OF A SIX-HUNDRED-ACRE FARM

The focal point of the Truman farm when Harry Truman returned was the home that his grandmother and uncle rebuilt after the 1894 fire. The home was probably constructed in phases after the fire and was painted white and trimmed in green. A kitchen is located at the rear of the building, attached to a dining room that had a desk located in one corner. Truman probably kept his farm journals and completed other clerical work at this desk. It was also from this desk that he would write many letters to his high school sweetheart, Bess Wallace. Above the dining room was a small bedroom, accessible by a narrow set of stairs. Harry Truman shared that bedroom with his brother, Vivian, and the hired hands who frequented the farm. Truman remembered, "The hired man stayed all night and has the fresh air habit to an extreme. He had all the windows in the room skyhigh. I piled on some additional covers but I nearly shook the bed to pieces before I got warm."[28] There is some evidence to suggest that the small kitchen, the dining room and the one bedroom upstairs were built quickly, and the front part of the house was constructed later.

Coming back down the narrow staircase that led to Truman's room and entering the dining room once more, a visitor to the home would have to step up to enter a short hallway that leads to the front portion of the house. If the visitor exited the house through the front door, he could see the row of maple trees that Truman's grandfather and mother planted in 1868. Also located on the wall by the front door was probably a telephone. On either side of the hallway are two rooms. On the north side is the parlor where Truman's mother liked to read. On the south side is the sitting room where family members, including Truman, enjoyed

View of the farm, circa 1900. *Truman Library.*

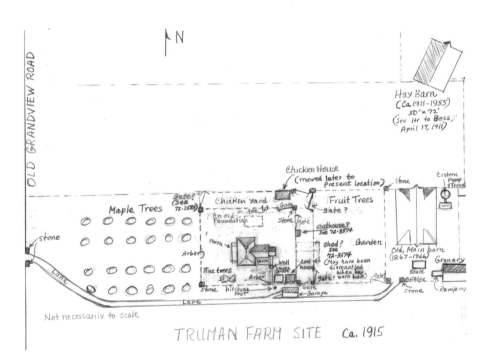

Hand-drawn map by Neil Johnson of how Fred Truman, son of Vivian, remembered the Truman farm. *Grandview Farm vertical file, Truman Library.*

Martha Ellen Truman, Harry Truman and Harriet Young (seated) at the farm, circa 1906.
Truman Library.

conversation. Above the parlor and sitting room are two bedrooms that
are easily accessible from a staircase leading upstairs from the central hall.
Truman's grandmother, father, mother and sister used these bedrooms
when they were on the farm; however, Harry Truman's bedroom did not
connect in any way with these two bedrooms.

When Harry Truman stepped out onto the front porch, he would have seen
the maple grove, which extended to the west past Blue Ridge Boulevard to
Grandview Road, where two round stone pillars marked the entrance to the
farm. Just to the south of these stone pillars is the old cemetery, where Harry
Truman dug at least one grave. Truman wrote:

> *This morning I was helping to dig a grave. It is not nearly such a sad
> proceeding as you'd think. There were six or seven of us, and we'd take
> turns at digging. Those who weren't digging would sit around and tell the
> one who was how it ought to be done and tell lies about the holes they'd
> dug and the hogs they'd raised. We spent a very pleasant forenoon and then
> went to the funeral. It was a Christian Science funeral. I never saw one
> before. They are very impressive. You know we have a cemetery in our front*

The cemetery where Harry Truman dug graves. *Photo by author.*

The farm lane. *Truman Library.*

yard and some of us usually get to help dig the graves. Our front yard is a quarter of a mile long and about half as wide so you see there is room for the cemetery without crowding.[29]

On another occasion, Truman recalled getting the farm lane gates and the cemetery gates reversed after coming home from Independence late at night, and he remarked:

That cemetery is the best behaved I ever heard tell of. I have been passing it at midnight and 1:00 A.M. since 1906 and never have I seen even so much as one piece of sod turn over or one gravestone behave other than it should. It's the live ones I'm scared of.[30]

If Truman returned to the main house from the cemetery, he would have walked up the lane, which, as he said, was about a quarter of a mile long from the entrance to the home. In 1914, he would have found a garage at the end of the lane for his 1911 Stafford automobile, and just to the left of the garage, he would have remembered a pump that he painted white after running into it one dark night. The pump replaced a well that was present when Harry Truman arrived in 1906.[31] Proceeding on into the backyard, and just to the north, Truman would have seen the fifty- by seventy-two-foot hay barn that was finished in the summer of 1911 and also the main barn that Solomon Young constructed in 1868, which measured forty-five by seventy feet and was located almost behind the 1894 home, just to the south of the hay barn.[32] One newspaper article noted that the barn was painted red and was constructed with sturdy walnut square posts and beams, and the "pens and stalls lined the east and west walls and a large pen filled its interior." The article also noted that a "substantial loft" stood above the stalls and pen.[33] The main barn burned in the 1960s, and the hay barn was removed in 1955.[34] Just to the south of the main barn stood the granary, which was also red.

The farm also had a number of other outbuildings, including an outhouse, since there was no running water in the home, a smokehouse and a chicken house. Harry Truman recalled that about forty or fifty feet behind the main house, there was a smokehouse, "with storage wings on each side," and just behind that was the icehouse.[35] The farm buildings were connected by a series of lanes that were fenced off and marked by stone pillars (some of the pillars are still located on the farm property). Usually, some type of fence surrounded the farm home to keep the farm animals away from the main house.

The barn that
Solomon Young built.
Truman Library.

Interior photo of the main barn, taken in the 1960s. *Truman Library*.

Right: Mary Jane Truman at the farm well. *Truman Library*.

Below: Martha Ellen Truman at the pump. *Truman Library*.

The neighborhood surrounding the Truman farm had witnessed a number of changes since the arrival of Solomon Young. For the most part, southerners had settled the area, and that would not change until after the Civil War. They had come to the edge of the frontier and, like Solomon Young, had participated in the settling of the West through their freighting operations. Others, like Elijah Slaughter or John R. Jones, had come before the Civil War and decided to homestead the area. If the average size of a Missouri farm when Harry Truman farmed was 125 acres, it follows that Truman and his neighbors were no average farmers. There were several neighboring farms that had over 100 acres; however, the Truman farm was one of the largest in the area. Why? The answer can partly be found in the fact that Solomon Young earned a very good income as a freighter along the trails, and when he returned to Jackson County after his westward adventures, he invested most of his profits into purchasing land, which the family held on to into the twentieth century.

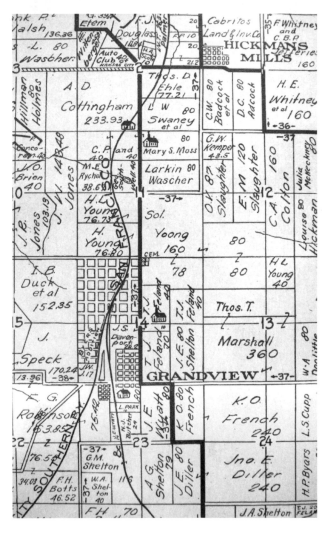

1911 plat map. *Photo by author.*

Anatomy of a Six-Hundred-Acre Farm

When the Civil War came, the area was rocked by violence, and the Youngs and Slaughters temporarily vacated their farmsteads and returned after the war. However, after the war, the neighborhood had at least one family who was not from the South: the Coltons. By the time Truman moved in, it was somewhat of a study in contrasts. Prior to 1900, the area around the Young/Truman farm featured freighters and pioneers like the Youngs and Slaughters. Just to the north of the Truman farm stood the Slaughter farm. Elijah. F Slaughter, who was born in Washington County, Tennessee, grew up in Kentucky before his family came to Jackson County in 1852, and he settled in Washington Township by 1870. His son, Orlando Vinton Slaughter, was born in 1854, and he farmed the place after his father died in 1902. O.V. Slaughter's son, Stephen S. Slaughter, was a contemporary of Harry Truman, and he remembered:

> Up to 1906 on our farm…we had no phone, no electricity, no gas or electric lights, no auto, no tractor, no plumbing, indoors or out, no central heating. We heated the house and cooked with a wood or a coal stove, we got our water from the spring or the cistern, we read by the light of coal oil lamp.[36]

Like the Youngs, who had suffered during the Civil War, the 1920 *History of Jackson County Missouri* noted that Elijah had also "lost heavily during the Civil War." The history noted that Elijah had purchased the farm north of the Youngs in 1895 and had taken to breeding and raising dairy cattle. The history continued:

> He has a well improved place which is well equipped with a special view of carrying on dairying by the most modern approved methods. His dairy barn is calculated to accommodate about 30 head of milch [sic] cows. He sells the product of his dairy, which consists of cream, in Kansas City.

The biographical sketch concluded by noting, "Mr. Slaughter is a Democrat and a member of the Christian church. He is one of Jackson County's substantial citizens and is public spirited and progressive."[37]

After Elijah died in 1902, O.V. Slaughter continued to manage the dairy operation until the 1920s; however, he also founded the Grandview Bank in 1907 and actively participated in the Jackson County Farm Bureau, which was founded in 1913.[38] Harry Truman also became involved in the Farm Bureau; however, he did not frequent the Grandview Bank. Instead, he favored a bank in Belton operated by Frank Blair, a Masonic friend. Perhaps

O.V. Slaughter's bank in Grandview. *Truman Library*.

the reason Truman favored the bank in Belton can be found in the fact that the Slaughters never joined the Masonic organization. Still, the Trumans and Slaughters were close—so close, in fact, that when Harry Truman ran for his first elected office as Eastern County judge in 1922, he successfully appealed to O.V. Slaughter to chair one of the first meetings where Truman discussed his candidacy.[39]

Like Solomon Young and O.V. Slaughter, John R. Jones hailed from a southern state—North Carolina. His family came to Missouri in 1845, and after he married in 1856, he settled on a farm in Jackson County. In 1858, he purchased land on the western boundary of the Young/Truman farm. An 1896 history noted that Jones supported the Democratic Party, was a member of the Baptist Church at Grandview and, during the Civil War, served as a "private in Frank McKinney's company, under Colonel Rosser." Like the Youngs and Slaughters, the biographical sketch noted that "he and his family were subjected to losses and trials incident to life along the border in those troublous [*sic*] days."[40]

Another neighbor to the northeast of the Young/Truman farm was C.A. Colton, who in 1911 owned 160 acres of land just to the immediate east of the Slaughter property. Cora Adell Miller Colton's family came to Jackson

J.C. Jones Lumber receipt. *Papers of Mary Jane Truman, Truman Library.*

County in 1884 from Bedford, Indiana. She married James B. Colton in 1890. Colton, from Pennsylvania, had come to Jackson County in 1878 and settled in the Hickman's Mill area. The 1920 *History of Jackson County* called Mr. Colton "a leading farmer and stockman of Washington township" and noted that "Mr. Colton is a Republican and he and Mrs. Colton are members of the Christian church."[41]

As previously mentioned, for the most part, Truman's neighbors were individuals who owned larger farms than the average Missouri farmer, were predominately from the South and had settled in the area prior to the Civil War. Harry Truman and his father also did business with many of the Grandview merchants, including J.C. Cagley, general blacksmithing and woodworking; Lindsay and Vest Hardware, tinware, nails, wire, stoves and feed; and W. W. Storry General Grocery and Meat Market, all of Grandview, as well as the J.C. Jones Lumber Company, which had locations in Grandview and Hickman Mills.[42]

3

J.A. TRUMAN & SON, FARMERS

People out here are kidding me about following in the footsteps of my father. They say I do it in an altogether too literal manner.[43]

From 1910 to July 1917, Harry Truman exchanged 230 letters with Bess Wallace in Independence. The letters revealed the seasons of farm life on a six-hundred-acre farm, as well as the challenges. The challenges included the weather and working with all the farm animals—horses, mules, hogs and cattle. The horses and mules provided the power on the farm because tractors were not used in the farming operation. Another challenge included finding and retaining hired men. Vivian left the farm in 1911, when he married, and working such a sizeable farm required significant human power beyond just that of Harriet Young, Martha Truman, John A. Truman, Mary Jane Truman and Harry Truman. Managing the farm required that the Trumans use hired hands, and finding good hired hands—and retaining them—was a constant challenge. Another challenge was that although the Young/ Truman farm was successful in producing crops and grazing cattle sold in the Kansas City market, a lawsuit clouded the financial future of the farm and the financial future of Harry Truman. Finally, one of the most significant struggles Truman faced as a farmer was the death of his father. Harry always thought that his father made the farm run, and he found managing the farm difficult without the older man's presence.

Truman recalled the cycles of planting and harvesting on the farm on two separate occasions. The following selections reveal that the Truman farm practiced crop rotation, which, according to Truman, significantly increased farm production; however, it is not clear where the impetus for the crop rotation came from—Harry Truman or his father. In one of the letters to Bess, Harry Truman wrote:

> *Papa is reading the farm press aloud for my benefit. I haven't heard a word for ten minutes. He always stops and asks what I think when some exceptionally large lie has been read. The farm papers are run for the advertising money and not for the subscriber. Their farm opinions are mostly rot. They'll tell some long-winded tale about the great record some guy has made feeding cattle and at the end you'll find that he's only fed three and that took all his time and a hired man's. What we want to know is how to feed a carload and not have anything to do.*

The Farm Bureau did not establish a presence in Jackson County until 1913, and Harry Truman did join the organization, but according to Truman's own diagrams, the crop rotation started in 1911.[44] An article in the 1945 *Prairie Farmer* revealed that prior to Harry Truman's arrival at the farm, his father had operated it "as more or less of a stop-over place for the stock he bought and sold." The article continued, "One of Harry's first moves after he took over supervision of the farm was to start a system of farm record books." A neighbor recalled that Harry Truman "spent every spare moment readin' or figurin'."[45] When Vivian left the Young/Truman farm in 1911, Harry and his father created J.A. Truman & Son, and the name suggested that both brought their unique skills to the table. John A.

Papers of Mary Jane Truman, Truman Library.

Truman brought his extensive knowledge of livestock and trading, and his son brought his focus on experimenting with efficient farming practices.

Harry Truman remembered his farming experience in the following way:

Well, I went to the farm in 1906 and stayed there, contrary to all the prophecies, until April 1917, really until August 5, 1917. It was a great experience. Wish I'd kept a diary. It was my job to help my father and brother feed the livestock, sometimes milk a couple of cows, then help my mother get breakfast. After breakfast we'd go to the fields. In spring and fall there'd be plowing to do. We had gang plows made by the Emerson Plow Company—two twelve-inch plows on a three-wheeled frame. It required four horses or mules to pull it and if an early start was had, about five acres could be broken up in a day—not an eight-hour one but in, say, ten or twelve hours. In the spring when the weather was cool and the teams could be kept moving the time was shorter. That sort of plow is the best demonstration of horsepower, pounds, feet, minutes. Sometimes the horses gave out and then the power was off until a rest was had. Riding one of these plows all day, day after day, gives one time to think. I've settled all the ills of mankind in one way and another while riding along seeing that each animal pulled his part of the load. Sometimes in the early part of the year it would be so cold that walking was in order to keep warm, even when a sweater, two coats and an overcoat were worn.

It was always my job to plant the corn, sow the wheat and run the binder to cut the wheat and oats. I usually pitched hay up to my father on the stack also. My father hated a crooked corn row or a skipped place in a wheat field. We had no crooked rows and our wheat and oat fields had no bare places in them and when the binder had finished a wheat or oat field there were no uncut strips in the field. We used a crop rotation system in our farm program. We'd plant corn after clover. Starting with wheat we'd sow clover on the wheat field in the spring and usually get a crop of clover hay that fall. The next year we'd spread all the manure from the farm and the little town adjoining it on the clover field. Nearly every family in the little town of 300 people had a cow or two and a horse. My father and I bought a manure spreader and kept it busy all the time when we were not doing other necessary things. We'd break the clover field up in the fall and plant corn the next spring, sow oats in the corn stubble the next spring and wheat after oats. It would take five years to make the complete rotation but it worked most successfully. We increased the wheat yield from thirteen to nineteen bushels—the oats from eight to fifty bushels and the corn from thirty-five to seventy bushels to the acre. Besides these increased yields in

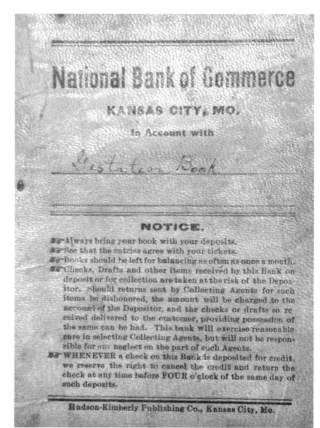

Above: Harry Truman on a cultivator. *Truman Library*.

Right: Harry Truman's gestation book. *Papers of Mary Jane Truman, Truman Library*.

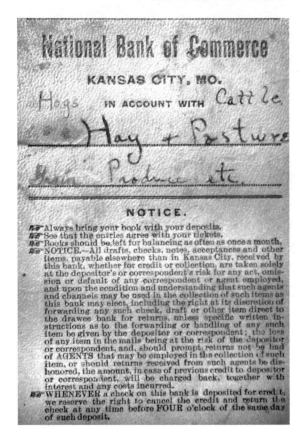

Harry Truman's hay and pasture book. *Papers of Mary Jane Truman, Truman Library*.

the grain crops we always had two excellent hay crops and at least one seed crop from the clover, so my practical education in farm management took place in those ten years.[46]

On another occasion, he remembered:

I studied soil improvement and farm management. Did everything on the farm that was necessary to be done from being a midwife to an old sow in the middle of the night, to helping a wild heifer have her calf. We had riding plows, two 12 inch moldboards on a three wheeled frame, pulled by four horses or mules or two of each.

The big wheel on the land [sic] side was just nine feet in circumference. I had a mark on it so I could count the revolutions so you see I could tell exactly how much plowing was done in 12 or 14 hours. It was usually about five or six acres. For five acres it took about 10 hours at 2½ miles an hour.

Then after the field was plowed and harrowed in the fall along in September wheat was sowed with a 12 disc drill which covered eight feet. I had a marker on the drill so that no skipped places would appear when the wheat came up. Those drilled wheat rows were as straight as the corn rows in the spring when corn was planted.

When wheat was ripe in July it was cut with an 8 foot binder shocked and sometime later threshed. Usually clover was sown on the wheat and a crop of stubble and clover would be cut in the fall and the next year a fine crop of hay and a clover seed crop would be harvested. After a year or two fall plowing would prepare the field for corn the next year. When corn was gathered the stalk field was used as pasture all winter and then the stalks were cut up and oats would be sown and then after fall plowing, wheat and the rotation. It worked

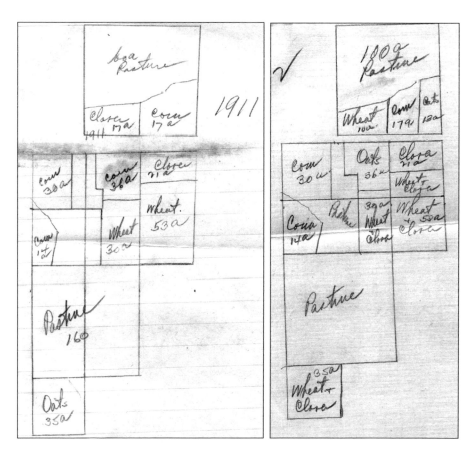

Above left: Truman's 1911 crop rotation map. *Papers of Mary Jane Truman, Truman Library.*

Above right: Truman's 1912 crop rotation map. *Papers of Mary Jane Truman, Truman Library.*

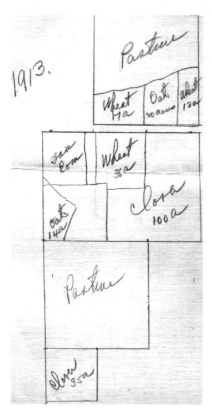

Truman's 1913 crop rotation map. *Papers of Mary Jane Truman, Truman Library.*

fine and more than doubled the yield for all crops. We'd have manure from the barns and from the stables in the little town up the road. It was a great life for ten years and then my father died and my brother left home and married.[47]

One of the busiest times of the year was during the month of July—threshing season. Threshing wheat required a significant expenditure of human and machine power. To say it was labor-intensive was putting it mildly. When the threshing machine arrived, the Truman farm was alive with activity both in the field and within the farm household. Most farmers did not own their own threshing machines. They would rent the machine; however, because the work was so intensive and required additional labor beyond hired help, each neighbor would take turns helping the others until the job was done.

Truman described the scene for Bess in the following manner:

His Majesty's reign has begun for us. The thresher arrived this evening, after supper *thank goodness. We will have men and boys roosting from*

L.C. Hall's threshing crew on the Truman farm. *Truman Library*.

L.C. Hall's threshing crew. *Truman Library*.

cellar to roof (we have no attic) and over the front yard too. I helped the owner of the machine thresh his own wheat this afternoon.[48]

Truman would frequently use the phrase "His Majesty" as a code word for the devil to describe an adverse situation.

The owner of the threshing machine Truman used was probably L.C. Hall, who had moved to Grandview in 1909. Hall was born in Kentucky in 1863 and he not only made a living by renting his Advance Rumley threshing machine out to the neighboring farmers, but he also operated a sawmill that produced walnut lumber. Like Truman, Hall was a Mason.[49]

Threshing also meant that the women in the household, Martha Ellen and Mary Jane, had to work extra hard because they were responsible for feeding all the additional workers. Mary Jane remembered:

You worked harder and we always had a big bunch of men at threshing time. We had as many maybe as 25 or 30 for dinner. In the wheat shucking and at the threshing time. You see, you had to have drivers for the wagons and then to load the wagons and it just took more. Well, you always had to have

Harry Truman's threshing receipt with L.C. Hall. *Papers of Mary Jane Truman, Truman Library.*

plenty of meat and plenty of potatoes and plenty of vegetables. Usually you had three or four vegetables and then plenty of meat and bread. Sometimes you could get the bakery bread and sometimes you couldn't; then you had to make biscuits or cornbread or something like that. Then there were the machine men; there would be five with a machine and they stayed overnight. So you had breakfast, dinner, and supper for them. Then at the noon meal the neighbors would come in; they traded work. We would have anywhere from 25 to 30, and we always had company besides. We always had a houseful.[50]

Harry Truman also noted that the threshing machine and inexperienced workers could bring the whole threshing operation to a quick halt. Writing to Bess in 1912, he said:

It wouldn't be any trouble to thresh if the bloomin' thing would run... Just as we get to going and the thing begins to behave, why some pinhead with a young team will run into the belt and throw it or dislocate some of the innards of the thresher itself by backing into it. Both happened today. I didn't happen to be the pinhead either time. If that doesn't happen, some gink who is tired will throw a half-dozen bundles in the seemingly insatiable maw and choke her down. Then it's time for the owner to cuss and the engine to buck and snort. Any blockhead can choke a machine, but it takes a smart man to feed it all it'll eat and still go a very rapid gait. I am not one of those, but Booney [one of Truman's hired hands] *is.[51]*

In addition to challenges from farming equipment and inexperienced workers, Harry Truman also struggled to work with all the animals on the farm. Horses and mules provided power and were used primarily to plow, disc, harrow and harvest the crops. Their presence was integral to the success of the farm, and knowing how to get them to perform their tasks was a challenge. Writing to Bess in 1911, Truman described in detail the different characteristics of his draft animals and what they required to get them to cooperate:

You see I have been sowing oats all week, got done Thursday night, and hauled about six tons of hay yesterday. My face is a sight, as the girls say. You know the wind blew something "fierce" last Tuesday and Wednesday and the sun also had some effect. Between them I look like raw beef or a confirmed "booze fighter." My voice is also somewhat weary from yelling at the horses. You know we drive four plugs to a drill—have them abreast.

It is an impossibility to have four with inclinations alike. I had four whose names may be some index to their character—William, Samuel, Jane, and X.X is a bronc—if you know what that is—and he has an insane desire to arrive at the other end of the field in the shortest possible time. You dare not touch him with a whip or let him hear one if you can help. William—Bill we call him of course—is an ex-buggy horse. He hasn't much idea of work but to get out of it if he can. I yell at him in my sleep sometimes. When I am not hallooing "Bill, Bill, go on," I am saying the same to Sam. Sam is a very large ex-dray horse and he never hurries under any consideration unless I poke him with a sharp stick or land on him with a baling wire whip. Jane, as Mrs. Barclay would say, is just right. She goes as she should. Well when I land on Sam and Bill, Jane and X want to run away. So I have to take it out in lung work and unprintable names. You can just bet that I am glad I'm done. I always sow Vivian's and mine too. This time I sowed seventy acres in five days. That is moving some. Vivian is well and has been hauling hay for me while I sowed his oats.[52]

Writing to Bess in 1911, Truman said, "A horse when he is hitched to a cultivator can make a religious crank use profanity. It is not possible to reach him as your hands are full holding the plow, so you have to take it out in strong talk."[53]

In 1912, he wrote:

Papa stacked hay today and didn't feel like doing the job was why I did it. You see, the rake is not quite so strenuous. He wouldn't let me do the stacking, though, and he positively won't run the rake. It is a cussin' job. Ours is one of the kind where the horses are hitched behind the rake. If you desire to go to the right, it is necessary to make the left hand horse move and the right one stand still. It works like the tiller on a boat—wrong end too. Sometimes you aim for a pile of hay and get one some distance away. I have arrived at the stage where I can generally go where I'm looking, therefore it's my job.[54]

Working with the farm animals was dangerous. On two separate occasions, both Harry Truman and his father suffered broken bones after rough encounters. The broken bones put each man out of commission and dealt a blow to the farming operation because there was no one to step into their places and fulfill their duties. In May 1911, a calf bucked Harry Truman to the ground and broke his leg. He wrote to Bess:

Speaking of that calf. It had the impudence to come up and look at me through the window a day or two ago and then kick up and bawl, as much as to say, "See what he got for monkeying with the bandwagon." He had three or four more calves of his own age with him. I have the sincere satisfaction of knowing that he will someday grace a platter—perhaps my very own…Calves are like men, some have sense—and some have not. Evidently he has not as he can never find his meals unless someone is kind enough to assist him. Even then he's ungrateful, as behold what he did to me. I only grabbed his tail and made a wild grab for his ear in order to guide him around properly when he stuck his head between my legs, backed me into the center of the lot, and when I went to get off threw me over his head with a buck and bawl and went off seemingly satisfied, I guess, for I didn't look.[55]

Although Truman was pleased that he did not have to complete his farm chores, he soon grew tired of walking on crutches. In a subsequent letter, he told Bess, "I am so crazy to walk I don't know what to do. I have been buggy riding a time or two and can go around on three legs. I am like the mathematical dog. I put down three and carry one. That infernal calf is veal now."[56]

By the time Harry Truman healed, John A. Truman had his own encounter with a horse that resulted in another broken bone, and Truman told Bess all about it:

Do you know I believed His Majesty himself has a special grudge against us. A horse fell on Papa Tuesday and broke one of the small bones in his left foot. He will be laid up for a month the M.D. says. I suppose as soon as he gets around again I'll take another turn. I am going to have the blacksmith make me some cast iron shoes and sox. They will name us the Insurance Grabbers Association sure now. Don't ever take out any accident insurance. Things begin to happen at once when you do. We'd worried along all our lives without any [insurance] and a certain gentleman with a large vocabulary and a bent for using it roped us last December. We've been having accidents in job lots since. I really don't know but what those polices had something to do with the dry year.[57]

According to an article in the *Prairie Farmer*, Truman began to focus on raising particular breeds of livestock instead of trying to trade in every kind of livestock, a practice in which his father had considerable skill. The article noted that "his real love in livestock was Hampshire hogs" and that "it was

Registry papers for Don. *Papers of Mary Jane Truman, Truman Library.*

not surprising that he did pick one breed and buy the best sows and boar he could find, for during his youth his father's feed lot had held a strange conglomeration of many breeds with few if any purebreds."[58] However, working with hogs was challenging, and they were also subject to disease. Still, as Truman noted, they were important to the profitability of the farm:

> *I have been to the lot and put about a hundred rings in half as many hogs' noses. You really haven't any idea what a soul-stirring job it is, especially on a day when the mud is knee deep about the consistency of cake dough. Every hog's voice is pitched in a different key and about time you get used to a squeal pitched in G minor that hog has to be loosed and the next one is in A-flat. This makes a violent discord and is very hard on the nerves of a high-strung person. It is very much harder on the hogs' nerves. We have a patent shoot (chute maybe) which takes mister hog right behind the ears and he has to stand and let his nose be bejeweled to any extent the ringer sees fit.*
>
> *I don't like to do it, but when a nice bluegrass pasture is at stake I'd carve the whole hog tribe to small bits rather than see it ruined. Besides it only hurts them for about an hour and about one in every three loses his*

rings inside of a week and has to endure the agony over again. If someone would invent a hog that wouldn't root he'd be a benefactor to suffering farmers and a multimillionaire in no time. I hate hogs myself except in the form of ham, sausage, and bacon, but they bring the dollars faster than anything else on a farm, so they're a necessary evil.[59]

On another occasion, he told Bess:

I haven't been much warmer since I sat on Mr. Slaughter's hogs while they were being vaccinated. He had some weighing about two hundred and as strong as mules. It was necessary to sneak up and grab a hind leg, then hold on until someone else got another hold wherever he could, and then proceed to throw Mr. hog and sit on him while he got what the Mo. University says is good for him…I helped at that job all morning Saturday and was supposed to get back this morning and finish. Maybe you think I wasn't glad when I called up and found out he'd done the job yesterday without my assistance.[60]

On yet another occasion, he wrote to Bess:

After breakfast I officiated at the burial of five hogs, dumping the whole works into one hole and one ceremony. Thank goodness there are only about a dozen left. We sent thirteen healthy ones to market this morning. When the dozen die, then our hog population will be zero, from ninety to start.[61]

In 1913, Truman described another challenging encounter with his hog population:

We shipped some cattle and sold some and also sold some hogs. The whole works had to be delivered in Grandview by noon and it was a rush to get there. Of course the hogs had to cause all the trouble they were able to. You know, it's a hard and fast rule that a hog's head is always turned opposite the way he is to go. There were twenty-nine to be loaded. I tried to get them in the barn and did get fifteen in. Usually when I have the barn door open and don't want them in every one of them will be right there. We loaded the fifteen and then tried to get the others in. I put some corn in the barn, and they all went in when one extra smart one grabbed an ear and ran out between my legs before I could shut the door. I went down without a struggle and the hogs all ran out. I finally got them in a little pen and when Papa came back we loaded them without any more trouble.[62]

Six days later, he wrote:

> *We killed hogs Thursday, and it is necessary to put the sausage into sacks and hang it this morning. That is always my job. Mamma always wants to do it but when she does, it makes her sick. Mary and Papa won't so it falls to me. I usually get sausage in my shoes, on my clothes, and in my hair, and over the kitchen floor. It isn't an agreeable job at all. But the sausage is worth the trouble later when it comes time to eat it. Then I am absolutely sure there's nothing in it but hog and the dirt off my own hands...I sold fifty pounds and Papa sold seventy-five. That leaves us fifty still, and I don't suppose we'll more than use it up before it ought to be, especially if it turns a little bit warm.*[63]

Years later, in 1951, Truman vividly recalled this process after the solicitor general sent him some "old-fashioned sausage," but the rendering of sausage had been a Truman family affair ever since he was a child:

> *I can remember on the farm in Missouri when I was a very small child how my mother and grandmother worked over the sausage and the rendering of the lard. They had a recipe for rendering lard that caused it to become just as white as snow and to keep forever. They stored it in large tin cans and fixed it, in those two jars you sent me, and then they would put the rest of it in sacks and smoke it with the hams and bacon. When I went back to the farm in 1906 we carried on the hog killing time just as our grandparents had done it but it is a lost art now. Even the so-called fancy Missouri hams are bought fresh from the packing houses and then cured. I certainly did appreciate your thoughtfulness in sending me the two jars of sausage which reminded me of times gone by.*[64]

Harry Truman was also partial to shorthorn cattle. According to Wayne Neely, who examined the *American Shorthorn Herd Book*, Truman's name first appeared in volume seventy-six, where he was listed as the owner of a red yearling bull, Lord Denham 2d 330450, which was bred by his neighbor, F.A. West of Belton. Neely concluded that "between April 1911 and December 1918 Harry Truman was a bona fide 'Shorthorn breeder.'"[65]

Although Truman does not specifically mention shorthorn cattle in his letters to Bess, there are a number of references made to milking, buying, selling and taking care of cattle:

Form 6

American Short-Horn Breeders' Association

CHICAGO, ILL., *July 13* 1911

Harry S Truman *Grandview* *Mo*

We have accepted for record for you......*1*......pedigrees in Volume......*79*......
American Short-Horn Herd Book, as follows:

Denham's Prince *352792*

SECRETARY

Clerk

NOTE. *We always certify to the party sending the money, unless otherwise instructed. Please notice if names are correctly given, notifying us at once of errors, that we may correct before being printed. The right of withdrawal is reserved in case of error or fraud being discovered.*

American Shorthorn Breeders Association registration papers. *Papers of Mary Jane Truman, Truman Library*

I haven't begun the 5:00 A.M. business yet, but I have gone to work. We are commencing at six now. But that's because we don't have to do anything but feed a dozen cows and twenty horses and about seventy hogs. I dug a load of fodder out of snow drifts three feet deep yesterday. Will do the same stunt in the morning and every one thereafter until the snow melts.[66]

There are two more that have to be milked after calves obtain a share. One of them is a most perverse creature. She has to have her feed in and you must approach her in a gentle and smiling mood. I always do until she's tied. It's "Whoa you nice cow. That's a nice cow," until the rope lands. Then it's "Now get away you blankety-blank speckled rip. Let's see you chase around the lot now." I make Mr. McBroom [hired hand] attend to her when I milk, which I don't very often.[67]

My dad arrived with his two loads of cows last night at seven o'clock. Mamma said he was on his ear in proper fashion when I wasn't there to meet him. He called me in the morning from Lowry City, [Missouri] and the K.C. Central had to repeat the message…We have more old cows now than you have chickens I guess. Fifty-two new ones and thirty we already had. It sounds like the stockyards on a busy day…Instead of being two hours night and morning tending to the cows it is now twelve hours all day.[68]

Papa's going to St. Clair County in the morning and says he's not coming back for three days! Ain't it awful. Just think of me arising at 5:00 a.m. and making three fires on these chilly mornings. Papa sleeps with a fire and so he doesn't mind starting another one. I sleep with the windows up and shake for thirty minutes every morning when there's a fire already going… What under the sun he wants to stay down there three days for I can't see. Perhaps he'll buy some more cows and string out the feeding process some more. It will be such a nice job while he's gone. The fodder is all covered with snow and it's a hard job to keep warm loading it. Generally I have snow up my sleeves and down my neck when Papa's on the wagon to pile it up. I guess I'll just pass up the fodder and feed hay while he's gone. There's a stack open and he'll never know the diff[erence]. Maybe the cows will. There's one thing, I'm not a gentleman farmer and if any of the cows get funny, they'll get a board instead of seeing my hat come off.[69]

After we got the cows fed, a man came and wanted to buy one for $42.50 and have us deliver her at Grandview. We told him that if we decided to take him up, we'd be there by two o'clock. The cow was caught after a half hour's tussle all over two acres, and we decided to weigh her and see how much we were being skinned. She was attached to the rear of a wagon and dragged on the scales. She weighed 930 and would bring about $54.00 in K.C. Papa decided that $10.00 was too much of a present to make so we turned her loose. I was mad as I could be after all that trouble, and then keep her. She's a horrid beast, always has her nose where she's not wanted. She's like Uncle Harry's four work steers. He said a fellow had two yoke of cattle named for the different churches. One was called Catholic, one Methodist, one Baptist and one Episcopalian. He had good reasons for calling them that too. He said the Episcopalian wouldn't eat at the proper time and would try to horn the rest away so they couldn't eat. The Catholic wanted all there was to eat and didn't want the rest to have any. The Methodist was always battling and wouldn't pull a pound, and the Baptist wanted to run and jump in every hole of water he saw. This cow is of the Catholic persuasion. It was 2:00 P.M. when the cow episode was finished.[70]

While the weather and the farm animals could be challenging for Truman, working with the hired hands could be equally as challenging. There seemed to always be one hired hand on the farm—usually two when the planting/threshing cycle began in the spring and continued through the fall. Sometimes the hired hands would spend the night, and if they did, they shared the bedroom with Truman located above the dining area. This bedroom did not connect with either Mary Jane's or Martha Ellen's bedrooms. The women of the household also had some help. Apparently, for a time, an African American woman assisted with the laundry.[71] Having the hired men also meant that Mary Jane and Martha Ellen cooked extra meals for them; however, sometimes Truman would cook breakfast and help out with the meals at threshing time.[72]

In 1911, he wrote to Bess:

> *We have some stock and I tell you it is some cold job to feed them every morning and night. I put as much off on the hired men as I possibly can, but still I have to get out every morning myself and feed the horses. Papa does the milking. I don't mind after I get out as it isn't cold to work, but my it's awful to start.*[73]

Having the hired men on the farm made it run. Specifically, after Vivian left in 1911, the hired men became an even more important component of the six-hundred-acre farm labor force, and they would become indispensable when Harry Truman became involved in a number of off-the-farm pursuits.

Truman became supervisor of the hired men when his father traveled the state in search of quality livestock. He told Bess:

> *Papa went to Joplin this evening and I am boss. I made one of the hired men stay all night so he can get up at 5:00 A.M. and help do the feeding. I had rather be stung for two meals than do all that tearing around by myself so early in the morning. I am getting to be real aristocratic. It will take all summer's hard work to purge my soul of last year's loaf. I hope I never have to loaf with the same excuse.*[74]

Finding the right hired men was tough, and Harry Truman was tough on them. In May 1913, he revealed to Bess, "We have the freshest hired man that ever hopped a clod. He has to know where every letter comes from and to whom every one goes."[75] He also told her in December of that year how he paid them:

> *The hired men are paid off. They beat me badly when I paid them. Wornall hadn't had a settlement since July. He had over forty dollars coming. The other fellow got thirty dollars. Just think what a lot of Christmas presents that would have bought.*[76]

In March 1914, Truman wrote to Bess:

> *The hired man is just now finishing up with the harrow. We thought we*
> *were going to lose him Sunday. I gave him $15 Saturday night and he said*
> *he was going to pay some bills he owed. I guess he must have hit a crap*
> *game first because he didn't get home until Sunday morning. He came up*
> *here about noon looking rather dilapidated and said his wife had given him*
> *a round with the poker. Said he guessed he'd have to leave as it looked as*
> *if he wasn't going to be able to stay home. I guess they must have patched*
> *things up because he hasn't said anything more about leaving. He's a great*
> *big man, and his wife won't weigh over a hundred pounds. I'm going to*
> *work your mother's system and pay on Monday after this. I wouldn't have*
> *this fellow leave for anything. He's the best man we ever had. Mamma is of*
> *the opinion that he needed braining, but there is always a bond of sympathy*
> *between women when a man has been shooting craps and every good man*
> *has his failings. I mean good hired men. Luke, for instance!*[77]

However, in April 1914, Truman informed Bess that "the man we hired is
a good one too, so I guess we'll have two for a month. Then the best one gets
to stay. I am hoping they'll manage to get along all right."[78] By May 1914,
there was trouble, and he informed Bess of the situation:

> *One of our hired men (the other one) is off on a toot. He's been gone since*
> *Saturday. He's drawn all that's coming to him too. Also it's all he'll ever*
> *draw I guess. No boozers for mine. Our hand of help is almost equal to*
> *Luke. First one and then the other has a tantrum. No man that's any good*
> *would be a farmhand, though, so it's not to be expected that good ones can*
> *be found. One good thing, they are plentiful and are not hard to break in.*[79]

When Truman's father fell ill in August 1914, he had to take on more farm
responsibilities, which meant he had to supervise the hired hands—the job
his father usually had and one in which the son struggled. Writing to Bess in
September 1914, he said:

> *To cap Tuesday off the hired men had a fuss and almost came to blows. I*
> *had to threaten to take a hand myself to restore peace. Today I put one of*
> *them to plowing in one place and the other in another place. They seemed*
> *to be rather ashamed of themselves this morning. If they'd fought, I'd have*
> *had to can them both and then wouldn't I have been in it.*[80]

J.A. Truman & Son, Farmers

In November 1914, John A. Truman, who had developed what was probably stomach cancer, died. This was a terrific blow to Harry Truman and to the farming operation. John's ability to judge the quality and weight of livestock had been integral to the farming operation, and so was his ability to motivate the hired hands to stay on task. Now, all of those duties fell to his son, who was overwhelmed. Harry turned to Bess, who attended the funeral at the farmhouse, for support and wrote to her soon after his father's death:[81]

> I have quite a job on my hands now trying to make things run as smoothly as they formerly did. You know, I've been in the habit of running the farm for some time, but Papa always made it go. He could make the men step lively even after he was sick a great deal better than I can or ever will. It surely makes me feel a loss that is quite irreparable, I tell you. There are things that I don't suppose I'll ever learn that were entirely natural to him. I have got to arrange to get some cattle to eat up a lot of feed I can't sell, and I'm morally certain that I'll be skinned on the deal. When Papa did those things, the other fellow was never sure that he had all his hide when the deal was over. About six weeks before he died he bought ten cows from an old tightwad here in the neighborhood that no one else can do business with for $500 and sold them for $900. If I could only make deals like that, there'd be nothing to worry about.
>
> It is probably a very good thing that I have more work to do than I can possibly get done because I have something else to think about.[82]

While Truman had to deal with his father's death in 1914, he also had, prior to John's death, struggled for several years to settle a lawsuit that had been brought by Harriet Young's children, who were not pleased that they were cut out of her estate when she died in 1909. Those children included the Bartleson and the Everhart families. According to Truman, the lawsuit cost the Trumans $100 a month in legal fees, which Truman believed threatened the financial stability of the farm.[83] Truman first mentioned the suit in 1911:

> This is a mighty poor Christmas letter but our dear relatives have succeeded in giving us the bluest Christmas since grandmother died. If you could see the allegations in the brief, you'd think my mother was the prime lady villain. It makes me so mad I could fight a boilermaker. They even accused our grandmother of being weak minded and most everything else—when she was the best businesswoman I ever expect to see. If we'd ever mentioned property to her, that itself would have finished us—as it should have done.[84]

In 1912, Truman wrote to Bess about the lawsuit and its financial impact on the farm:

> *If we can just settle our lawsuit, this farm will produce about six or seven thousand a year clear and that means about three more than that in town. Such things, though, take bushels of time and barrels of money…Our dear relatives may take the whole works yet and then we'll have to begin again. That sure would be awful, but I guess we'd live through it.*[85]

In 1913, the case continued to move along. Harry Truman traveled around with his lawyer, Fred Boxley, whom he had met while serving in the Missouri Guard, and collected testimony to support his mother and uncle's claim to all of the six hundred acres. In 1913, the case was heard before a jury, and Truman wrote to Bess:

> *You know I don't care for money nor appreciate its value when I have it, but the things that lawyers and some people will do to obtain a little of it are certainly astonishing. I have sincerely wished that Grandma had died a poor woman then we'd have seen who cared for her. Some of those stoneheaded Dutch on that jury argued that Mamma forced her to make a will in her favor and that her letters were merely saved for just such a contingency as this. They were also of the opinion that Mamma was mean to her sisters and kept them from going to see their mother. The more I think of it the worse I feel, and the more I feel like punching the heads of those old lawyers and the young Everharts. There really does not seem to be any use in a person trying to give his worldly goods to those he wants to have them. If he thinks he's going to die and deeds his property away he'll live to be ninety-nine years old and get kicked out by those he gave it to, and if he wills it some jackleg lawyer will leave a flaw in the will so he can halve the property with the heirs or divide it with the opposition lawyers. That's rather a pessimistic view but I know that if I could arrange an income of about six or seven hundred a month I don't believe I'd strive for any more money. I'd make it my business to spend that scientifically—and thoroughly. I believe I could make quite a number of people enjoy life on that much.*[86]

There were more deliberations over the lawsuit in November 1913, and Truman traveled to court to hear Grandma Young's children testify against his mother in court. He told Bess:

*I am hoping to see you Wednesday evening. I suppose Mamma and I will
have to be present at Aunt Susan's [Bartleson] grilling. If she'll only stick
to the truth I won't mind, but if she does like the rest I sure will hate to be
present. One hates to see a white-haired old lady, one he likes and respects,
tearing up the truth just for a few dollars. It has a tendency to make a
pessimist out of a person. I like money as well as anyone but I think I'd
do without it if I had to cast aspersions on my mother's character to get it.
I suppose you are tired of hearing me harp on our old suit but it means so
much to us if we lose that I can't help it.*[87]

Finally, in 1914, a settlement came on the lawsuit. Truman shared the
results with Bess in two separate letters:

*I'll have some title to this place when I turn the checks over. They're all
going to deed their shares to me, and I'm supposed to deed them over to
Mamma and Uncle Harry. I could just prosecute the suit to its termination
and then I'd own five-sevenths of the farm anyway. There have been enough
suits in the family to date so I'll just very meekly deed the thing over and let
it go at that. I think though that they ought to compensate me for my trouble
in some way. I haven't any notion of getting a cent but I'll be very well
satisfied if Mamma gets her farm, and then maybe I can do something for
myself. Four years of litigation have been some strain both physically and
financially. If Uncle Harry will only let me act as his agent in selling some
of his property, though, things will be fine.*[88]

*I succeeded in getting Uncle Harry to divide the farm with Mamma. I
guess he got somewhat the best of it but I'd rather that than fuss with him.
This family [has] had fusses enough for one generation. Uncle Harrison is
going to rent us his share just as he always has, and I don't suppose we'll
know it's divided unless he should happen to die.*[89]

While Harry Truman spent a considerable amount of his time working
on the farm, tending the farm books and looking for ways to improve the
financial stability of the farm, he also spent a significant amount of time off
the farm involved in a number of pursuits. The next two chapters closely
examine those off-the-farm pursuits.

4

PURSUITS OFF THE FARM

On Wednesday evening the W.M. has asked me to conduct a Lodge of Instruction, on Thursday evening as president of the Commercial Club I had to call a town meeting to get ready for the Township Fair, and on Saturday I have to call a meeting of the Woodmen to get them to donate their half to the farmers for their exhibition Tuesday. Ain't that an awful array for one pigheaded farmer to have in a November week? Especially when he'd rather be some twenty miles away on every single night. I'm hoping for a flood or snow or some other disaster to take place for I'm dying to come to Independence.[90]

While farm life for some might have been filled with much solitude, the only solitude Harry Truman had on the farm was during the monotony of plowing and planting, and even that monotonous time he used to his advantage. Surprisingly, Truman was involved in a number of off-the-farm pursuits. He served a stint in the Missouri National Guard, joined the Masons and found the time to speculate in land with family members and neighbors. He also joined the Farm Bureau, Grandview Commercial Club and Modern Woodmen; became postmaster of Grandview; and dabbled in local politics. His pursuits, particularly his devotion to the Masons and to his girlfriend, Bess Wallace, greatly encouraged him to purchase a car, which was a luxury for a farmer in the early 1900s.

MISSOURI NATIONAL GUARD

Before coming to the farm in 1906, Harry Truman enlisted as a private in Battery B, National Guard of Missouri, in June 1905. He was proud of his enlistment and rushed home in his new dark blue uniform. The uniform completely threw

Harry Truman in his Missouri
National Guard uniform.
Truman Library.

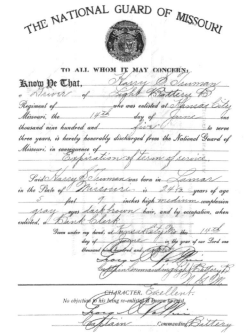

Harry Truman's National Guard
discharge certification. *Papers of
Mary Jane Truman, Truman Library*.

off his grandmother because her last encounter with a blue-uniformed officer during the Civil War had not gone very well. The Union forces had raided the farm during the Civil War, and Grandma Young told Truman, "Harry, this is the first time since 1863 that a blue uniform has been in this house. Don't bring it here again." Truman complied with his grandmother's wishes. Nevertheless Truman persisted in his commitment to the Missouri Guard, and he was appointed corporal in March 1906. He was discharged from his duties in June 1908, but a day later he reenlisted and was discharged in June 1911.

Truman described one of his National Guard experiences to Bess in the following manner:

> *A member of the Battery got his fingers connected with the breech block on one of those three-inch guns not long ago and left one of them in the gun. I think I shall quit the military stunt in June. My time is out then, I have been a member for six years and have had lots of fun, learned a little bit, and made some friends, so I guess I'd better quit while I am all in one piece. Out at Ft. Riley* [Kansas] *once while the outfit was out there, a shell exploded at the mouth of the gun and killed seven or eight who were standing too far front. So you see a person is not absolutely safe either in front or behind the gun.*[91]

MASONS

In 1908, a family member visited the farm, and Harry noticed a little pin he was wearing and wondered what it symbolized. On his next trip, the family member delivered an application for membership in Belton Lodge 450 Ancient Free and Accepted Masons. Truman filled out the application, and he was accepted for membership. He took his first degree in February, and by March he had finished his third. He was following in the footsteps of both his grandfathers, as they were Masons as well, and his brother, Vivian, who was also a member. Harry Truman practiced his Masonic lectures while he plowed the fields on the farm.[92] Truman defined Freemasonry as "a system of morals which makes it easier to live with your fellow man, whether he understands it or not."[93]

Because Grandview did not have its own lodge, Harry Truman wanted to start one—and he did. He obtained the necessary number of people to form a lodge, and in 1911, he became the presiding officer. He was later elected grand master in 1911. He was excited about the opportunity, and he expressed that excitement to Bess:

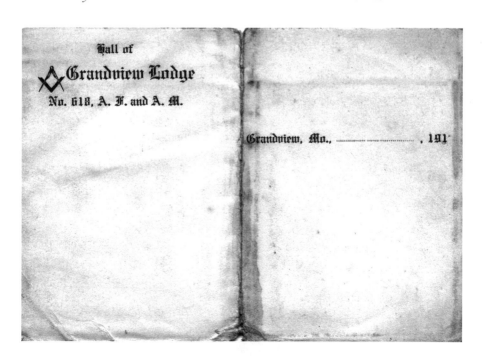

Right: Harry Truman's Belton Lodge Masonic Application, Belton (Missouri) Lodge No. 450, A.F. & A.M. Records, *Courtesy of the Belton Lodge and the Truman Library.*

Below: Papers of Mary Jane Truman, Truman Library.

A new Masonic Lodge is being organized at our town and they have given me the principal office. I have the big head terribly. The Deputy Grand Master was out to see us Wednesday night and handed me an awful lot of hot air. I haven't quite recovered from the effects yet.[94]

I have just heard that the Masonic Lodge I was telling you of is a success. There won't be two in our town. The one I belong to is in Belton six miles away. This one is in Grandview, only one mile.[95]

I have been working like Sam Hill on our Masonic Hall ever since I came home. We had our First Degree work last night and I conferred the first one that was put on. You see some time in the far distant future I'll be bragging about having performed that ceremony. There were about a dozen high moguls out from Kansas City and some from Belton. We had a good Ladies Aid Society time.[96]

Harry Truman served as grand master of the Grandview Lodge in 1912 and 1917. Mary Jane Truman became active in the Order of the Eastern Star, which was the Masonic equivalent for women, and throughout the remainder of their lives they were committed to both organizations.

Truman spent many hours of his precious free time attending Masonic meetings. Sometimes he was accompanied by his sister. His duties within the Masonic organization allowed him to develop fraternal bonds, but it was his first experience in developing relationships with a much wider body of contacts. This visibility had to have brought some political dividends later in life; however, it is not my contention that he joined the organization simply for political reasons. Writing in 1940, he noted:

Never in my career have I used either the Masonic organization or the Eastern Star to advance my political fortunes. You will find, I am sure, that the constitution of both organizations prohibits just such activities as you are proposing to put on. It will not only ruin the organization, but if you are not careful it will cause a split where no split should occur.[97]

One observer who examined the role of Truman's Masonic career concluded:

As a Freemason, Truman also learned the meaning of Brotherly Love, Relief and Truth. He put the first two into practice continually; Truth he continued to seek, which is a never-ending quest. He learned that time, patience and perseverance could accomplish almost anything. His understanding of Masonry's Cardinal Virtues—Temperance, Fortitude, Prudence and Justice—shows up throughout his life.[98]

While Truman embraced Freemasonry and its ideals, the letters that he sent to Bess also revealed his thoughts about race. His comments are disturbing, but they are part of the complexities of a person whose personal past was deeply rooted in southern culture. Writing to Bess in February 1914, he recalled the dream he had the night before, "I went nigger chasing again on Monday. Right through Central Africa: Vine St. There was no trace of that Nelson nigger. She has as completely disappeared as old Tom Swope's good qualities. Pretty far gone, isn't she?"[99] On another occasion, he wrote:

> I think one man is just as good as another so long as he's honest and decent and not a nigger or a Chinaman. Uncle Will says that the Lord made a white man from dust, a nigger from mud, then threw up what was left and it came down a Chinaman. He does hate Chinese and Japs. So do I. It is race prejudice I guess. But I am strongly of the opinion that negroes ought to be in Africa, yellow men in Asia, and white men in Europe and America.[100]

Truman spent a great deal of his off-the-farm time from 1910 until 1915 traveling to and from Masonic installations. He had grown very good at retaining and reciting the rituals, and his services were in demand, as attested to by the letter he sent to Bess:

> I have been dissipating this week in Pleasant Hill. The town is wet and I really could. The Grand Lecturer of Missouri was there and Mr. Blair wanted me to go learn a lecture for him! I have a hard enough head so that when anything is pounded into it in a strong manner, it stays. That's why I got called on.
>
> I am very glad I was, for one of the good old brothers down there took me home with him Tuesday night and gave me quail on toast for breakfast—all I could possibly hold, with a plate full of them still on the table when I left...This good brother begged me to stay Wednesday night, too, but I just had to come home. Papa says I only visit at home anyway. I am trying to make use of my time before we fire the hired men, for it'll be home for me then, sure enough. One reason why I attend these instruction Lodges is because when I visit K.C. lodges or Independence they make it a point to call on the farmer Master to do something—and if it is bungled they say, oh well he's from the woods; it's to be expected. If it isn't they won't believe I'm a farmer. I am though and I'm glad I am.[101]

The Scottish Rite has done its best to make a man of me, but they had such a grade of material to start with that they did a poor job I fear. It is the most impressive ceremony I ever saw or read of. If a man doesn't try to be better after seeing it, he has a screw loose somewhere.[102]

On two other occasions, Truman described his Masonic duties. He enjoyed the pomp and circumstance, the costumes and the ritual, but he noted it could be entertaining, too:

Vivian and I went to the dedication of the new Masonic Temple in K.C. last night. The Grand Master and all the big guns were out. The Grand Master always wears a tall plug hat and large gold jewel on his left breast. When he happened to be a large man he makes a very imposing figure, but a short one or a fat one is funny. The present one is tall and slim. With the high hat he looks to be about seven feet. But he's not as tall as I am when I got up against him last night. The one last year was a G.M. every inch. He was about six feet and weighed over two hundred. He had a foghorn voice, a young-looking face, and lots of gray hair.

They unwound yards and yards of pink tape last night and it was all very solemn. They always dedicate a Masonic Temple with corn, wine, and oil, pouring each one on with solemn invocations. This one is the finest in Missouri or most anywhere in the west. It is a York Rite Temple.[103]

I went down to Drexel last night with Mr. Blair and acted as assistant district lecturer. Went down on the K.C.S. and got back at 5:50 a.m. Got four hours sleep. You ought to see me teach blockheaded Masons how to talk. (Don't ever say that to anyone, for we don't admit that there are any of that kind.) They'd have to be blockheads if I taught them. We had lots of fun. There was a big, old fat guy present who got me tickled and I lost my high-and-mightiness in short order.[104]

Harry Truman was close to Frank Blair, a banker from Belton who had sponsored his application to the Masonic organization in 1909, and it was Blair who apparently saw some early talent in Truman's ability to conduct the Masonic meetings. Truman described Blair to Bess:

That is the reason I do business with Frank Blair. His doctrine is squeeze the rich ones and give the poor man a chance. He has the biggest country bank in western Missouri as a result too. He was in Grandview yesterday evening holding a Lodge of Instruction. He says every man has to have a hobby and his is Freemasonry, about as harmless alone as he could possibly have I guess. He says that the only trouble he has with his hobby is his wife getting after him for being away from home so many nights.[105]

His many absences to attend building dedications, Lodge of Instructions and conferral of degrees concerned his father. Truman wrote to Bess, "Papa is about to hire a substitute for me. He says I am losing interest in the farm… What I need is a sixty horse power motorcar. Then I could do a day's work and run around all night."[106]

LAND SPECULATOR

Throughout the time that Truman spent on the farm, he, like several of his neighbors and family members, was always looking for other opportunities for social and financial advancement. In particular, given the fact that the farm lawsuit had been ongoing from 1909 until 1914, and also the fact that during that time, Truman was seriously dating Bess Wallace and was trying to find a more stable work situation, it is no surprise that he was constantly looking for the next opportunity around the corner. In October 1911, he informed Bess, "There is a fellow who wants to go to South Dakota and register for a claim."[107] In the next letter, he informed her that he was headed to South Dakota with his cousin and a friend to examine some land opportunities, and he also explained what he thought he would find after arriving:

I bet there'll be more bohunks and "Rooshans" up there than white men. I think it is a disgrace to the country for those fellows to be in it. If they had only stopped immigration about twenty or thirty years ago, the good Americans could all have had plenty of land and we'd have been an agricultural country forever. You know as long as a country is one of that kind, people are more independent and make better citizens. When it is made up of factories and large cities it soon becomes depressed and makes classes among people. Every farmer thinks he's as good as the President or perhaps a little bit better. When a man works for a boss, he is soon impressed with how small he is and how great the boss is until he actually believes it is so and that money makes the world go round. It does I guess in very large cities.[108]

Apparently, nothing ever came of the South Dakota trip; however, in 1914 Truman wrote to Bess that he had "drawn No. 6199 at Ft. Peck" and that he would be traveling to Montana with Mr. Hall in May. Like the South Dakota trip, nothing ever came of this trip either.[109]

Even after the lawsuit was settled in 1914, Truman continued to look for other opportunities. In 1915 and 1916, he traveled to Texas, this time with Uncle Harrison, to look at land opportunities there. In 1916, en route to Fort Worth, he wrote to Bess:

> *We are approaching Ft. Worth an hour late…Uncle Harry seems to be enjoying himself. He is able to lead every big lie that is told in his presence by a bigger one. When he can do that he's happy. He's begun to cuss Texas though, which isn't so happy for me. I doubt very much if he allows me to do anything down here. If he doesn't, I'm going to try and make him loosen up at home. It is springtime here. They are plowing and burning just as we do in May. It is certainly fine weather down here. I want to stay but I can't. There's a month's work at home to be done in a week. Vivian and Mr. Blair seem to think that I am badly in need of a guardian for even suggesting west Texas. I have converted Blair but Vivian never. He can do nothing but quote his paw-in-law. You know the old geezer has just sold a one-third interest in a Joplin mine and made some more money. The mine cost the three of them $30,000. They sold it for $105,000. He has another one that brings him $1,000 a week. I wish him some more luck. That won't keep me from trying my luck if I can. You are well acquainted with my very urgent reasons for wanting some kind of good luck.*[110]

Pursuing these speculative land deals took him off the farm and, in particular, after his father's death in 1914, Truman's absence from the farm meant that the management of the farming operation fell to his mother and sister.

Farm Bureau

The Jackson County Farm Bureau was organized in 1913 prior to the passage of the Smith-Lever Act on May 8, 1914, which "provided for agricultural Extension work under cooperation between the agricultural colleges of the several states and the United States Department of Agriculture."[111] In 1913, Truman joined the Jackson County Farm Bureau, at the time under the leadership of E.A. Ikenberry. Ikenberry was responsible for dividing up the county into local farm bureaus organized by township. Soon, Truman became active in Washington Township, and in 1913 he served on a committee that organized the Washington Township Fair. He wrote to Bess:

> *I have the most awful job ahead of me you ever heard of. It is necessary for me to pay a visit to six country schools and make a speech at each one about the Washington Township Fair. It is going to be at Grandview and I am on the committee to get exhibits.*

He continued his letter by informing Bess that "Mr. Ikenberry is the man who is having the fair for the benefit of the farmers."[112]

In 1914, Truman told Bess that he was elected president of the Jackson County Farm Bureau, and he said the "job was wished on me without my knowledge. I wasn't even present when it was done."[113] It is unknown when he severed his ties with the farm bureau.

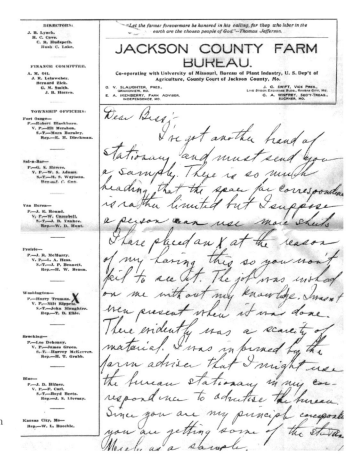

Jackson County Farm Bureau stationery.
Truman Library.

COMMERCIAL CLUB

At the same time Harry Truman was writing to Bess about this involvement in the farm bureau, he also mentioned that he was involved with the Grandview Commercial Club. The Commercial Club participated in the Washington Township Fair, and Truman told Bess that the club was "offering a prize for the school with the biggest attendance…Washington Township is trying to beat Prairie, which contains Lee's Summit. I hope we can."[114] He served as the club's president in 1913, but in January 1914, he informed Bess:

> *I have made up my mind to quit the Grandview Commercial Club because they sell booze and then, to be consistent, I join the K.C.A.C. [Kansas City Athletic Club] because they do! Most people are about that consistent in their actions. I'll try not to drink up all the K.C.A.C. has on draught the first time I go anyway.*[115]

Eight days later, he wrote Bess another letter about his involvement in the Grandview Commercial Club:

> *My mind is full of nothing but figures and double entries this afternoon. I have been spending the whole morning trying to get the books of the Commercial Club straightened out. They called on me to do it, and I'm going to resign from that club. I don't like the job or the club either for that matter. My official position ended January 1 anyway and I hoped to drop out without causing any disturbance, but they went and voted me an honorary life membership. Now I have to resign to get out. It doesn't please me to be tied up with a booze-selling crowd. I don't have any use for it. You never did see such a mess for a person to fix up as those books were. The fellow who helped me was thoroughly disgusted. We finally padded them with twenty-two dollars on the debit side and made them balance. He is going to quit same as I am and no one but us could find it, so I guess we're safe. Anyway the books prove to a penny.*[116]

MODERN WOODMEN

At about the same time Harry Truman became active in the farm bureau and the Grandview Commercial Club, he also joined the Modern Woodmen. The Modern Woodmen billed itself as a "fraternal life insurance Society for the whole family." Truman joined Camp 4311 in Grandview in 1911, and in 1913 and 1914, the membership elected him camp consul.[117] In January 1914, he told Bess:

> *I have to hold an instruction school tonight for the Woodmen. That is, I have to call it, the other boys [are] to do the instruction, because I'm not hunting learning any Woodmen foolishness. My head's nearly bursting open from the strain that's been put on it by the Masons, and that's a plenty for one rube.*[118]

AUTOMOBILE

When Truman began his courtship with Bess Wallace, one of the greatest obstacles to their relationship was distance. Even though only fifteen miles separated Grandview and Independence, it could take several hours if one traveled by horse and buggy between the towns. Also, when Truman's star rose within the Masonic organization, he needed a reliable form of transportation to get him to and from the installation ceremonies and building dedications; however, the farm lawsuit prevented the family from purchasing an automobile. That did not stop Harry Truman from talking about his need for an auto. Writing to Bess in January 1914, he said:

> *You may be sure that I would never want to waste an evening in sleep that could be spent at 219 Delaware Street. That's one reason I want an auto so badly. I could do a day's work and still arrive in your town at a reasonable hour. I suppose if I did have one, I'd learn to do my sleeping between stops. There's no doubt that it would not be worn out standing still.*[119]

In a subsequent letter to Bess, he wrote:

> *Ferson wants to sell me a Stafford car for $650. It's an old one but will outlast and outlook some of the new ones they are selling now. I told him that unless I could filch the amount from the Young estate while the settlement was being made there was no prospect of my owning a car. It sure is a bargain though. Uncle Harrison thinks we'll have to sell some of the farm, but I hope not. It will probably bring $200 an acre now but in four or five years it may be worth three times that. I hope I never have anything more to do with an estate like this one. It is a hoodoo from start to finish.*[120]

Harry Truman's Stafford automobile. *Truman Library*.

STATE OF MISSOURI
OFFICE OF THE SECRETARY OF STATE
1914
OWNER'S CERTIFICATE No. 39009
OF REGISTRATION

This Certifies that *Harry S. Truman* of *Grandview*, as owner of *30* h.p. Auto, made by *Stafford*, factory No. *24* type *Touring* has registered said Vehicle at p. *64*, Motor Vehicle Book *17*, and is Authorized to operate said Vehicle

Witness my hand and the Great Seal of State at Jefferson City this *23* day of *APR* *1914*. *Cornelius Roach*
SECY OF STATE

THIS REGISTRATION EXPIRES JANUARY 31, 1915.

Harry Truman's Stafford automobile license. *Papers of Mary Jane Truman, Truman Library*.

Finally, the farm lawsuit was settled by May 1914, and shortly before the settlement—and with full knowledge that the suit would probably be settled—Harry Truman persuaded his mother to either lend or give him the money to purchase an automobile. Truman wasted no time in acquiring the 1911 Stafford automobile for $600 in April 1914. Mary Jane Truman said that when her brother purchased the car, it was black, but he later painted it red. In 1953, Truman described the car as "a five-passenger open car with straps attached to the top that buckled to the front part of the frame, although it was usually driven as an open car. I had it remodeled into a hot sport roadster and took it to Camp Doniphan with me in 1917."[121]

Truman enjoyed the freedom that the car gave him, and he drove all over Jackson County. He even taught Mary Jane to drive. The car also enabled him to haul around members of his family, including the Noland cousins and Bess's brothers, George and Frank. They enjoyed going on picnics, fishing trips on the Little Blue and excursions to the Kansas City waterworks. Truman described his excursions to Bess:

> *I sure did take a drive Sunday evening—only ninety-seven miles after five o'clock. When we got home I thought I'd never want to drive anywhere again…Roads in Jackson County are becoming as familiar to me as the two blocks from Union to Delaware formerly were, and that's a fair acquaintance. I am getting so I don't object to driving like I did to begin with. Getting sort of used to it I suppose—five thousand miles in three months is moving around somewhat. That's one thousand miles more than Frank Blair went in three years.*[122]

There was one significant drawback to the Stafford, and that was the fact that only about three hundred of the cars were in existence. This made finding parts for them challenging and the repairs expensive. The papers of Mary Jane Truman are replete with receipts from the constant maintenance charges that Truman encountered. He described just what a challenge it was to hand crank the engine:

> *It almost jammed on me this morning. I had to spin it about ten minutes to make it go. The handle flew off the crank shaft and sprained my wrist and I bumped my head on the radiator. My chances of heaven get slimmer every day I have the thing if every cuss word is counted against me.*[123]

POLITICS

It was on the farm that Truman first gained knowledge of participating in the political process. He seemed to be interested in politics, but at times he was a reluctant and critical observer of politicians and the political process. In

1912 he told Bess that "politics is all he [Papa] advises me to neglect the farm for. I have other ideas. For instance, if I only owned a car, there'd probably be some very serious neglect."[124] In another letter to Bess, he remarked: "Politics are very bad for men's systems anyway."[125] In a subsequent letter, he expressed a rather jaded view of politics and politicians:

> *Politics sure is the ruination of many a good man. Between hot air and graft he usually loses not only his head but his money and friends as well. Still, if I were real rich I'd just as soon spend my money buying votes and offices as yachts and autos. Success seems to me to be merely a point of view anyway…To succeed financially man can't have any heart. To succeed politically he must be an egotist or a fool or a ward boss tool. To my notion, an ideal condition would be to have to work just enough so if you stopped you'd not go busted at once—but still you'd know if you didn't work you couldn't live. And then have your home and friends and pleasures regulated to your income, say a thousand a month. I am sure I'd be satisfied then to let vile ambition, political or monetary, starve at the gate.*[126]

He did enjoy following the politics of the day. In 1912, he talked about being one of William Jennings Bryan's "staunchest admirers," and he described his disappointment to her when farm work prevented his ability to listen to the speeches of Woodrow Wilson and fellow Missourian Bennett Champ Clark when both were seeking the Democratic nomination for the presidency in 1912.[127]

The Truman family entered the realm of politics when John Truman became road overseer in 1912 because he supported the eastern judge for Jackson County; judge repaid the favor by appointing John Truman as road overseer. The road overseer was responsible for collecting the poll tax, which was then used to pay for road improvements. Instead of paying the three-dollar poll tax, workers could agree to donate their time toward improving the roads in the township, and John Truman had to keep track of all this. When John Truman died, Harry Truman filled in for his dad, but the eastern judge changed political affiliations in 1916, and Harry Truman was out as road overseer.[128]

Truman also participated in the patronage system of politics when he asked his congressional representative, W.P. Borland, for his support to become postmaster of Grandview. He described the letter he sent to Congressman Borland as a "grand piece of political guff," and he told Bess, "I didn't ask

AT THE BOTTOM OF YOUR BALLOT WRITE THE NAMES
OF—

JOE H. BURDETT

—AND—

HARRY S. TRUMAN

For Democratic County Committee
WASHINGTON TOWNSHIP

Primaries, August 1, 1916.   127

Washington Township Democratic committeeman election. *Papers of Mary Jane Truman, Truman Library.*

him to appoint me straight out but asked him to make the appointment that the majority of the patrons of the office wanted."[129]

In all fairness, as Robert Ferrell recounts, Truman had to take a postal examination to be considered, and his scores were high, but to secure an appointment he also had to get congressional support. His top scores and congressional support paid off because he was appointed postmaster in December 1914. His term started in February 1915, but he did not do any of the work because he allowed a member of the Hall family, a widowed woman, to work the position and draw his salary. He resigned the position in 1915—the year he was in the midst of another off-the-farm pursuit as part owner of a mine in Commerce, Oklahoma.[130]

Truman maintained his commitment to civic duty when, in July 1916, he was appointed to fill out the term of a Hickman Mills Consolidated School District No. 1 school board member who had resigned. He continued his service on the board until May 1917, when he enlisted to serve in World War I. In his first election, in 1916, he ran for Democratic committeeman from Washington Township, but he lost in the August primary.[131]

5

THE COURTSHIP

I am hoping to see you Sunday and before if I can. It seems like a hollow week if I don't arrive at 219 Delaware at least one day in it.[132]

Given all of Truman's off-the-farm pursuits, it is hard to imagine that after 1910 he incorporated another duty to his increasing laundry list of pursuits—as boyfriend of one of his high school classmates, Bess Wallace. As Truman always told the story, he first saw Bess Wallace when they attended Sunday school at the First Presbyterian Church on Maple Street in Independence. While the two went to the same school, their social orbits were somewhat different. The Truman family had moved to Independence in 1890 to attend the community's excellent public school system. Bess's family had been in Independence since 1867. Her mother, Madge Gates Wallace, came from a wealthy Independence family, who came to Independence from the North during the Civil War and later started the Waggoner Gates Milling Company. In contrast, the Trumans, whose ancestors were southern, had bounced around southern Missouri and Grandview before they arrived in Independence in 1890. Living in Independence had to be quite a shock for the family patriarch John A. Truman, who earned most of his living as a farmer and a livestock trader.

Apparently, Harry and Bess did not date in high school, but their graduating class was so small that they did know each other. In 1900, shortly before Harry Truman graduated from Independence High School, he got a break in his relationship with Bess. His cousins, Mary and Ethel Noland, whose mother was a sister to John A. Truman, moved in across the street from the George Porterfield Gates home at 219 North Delaware. Bess lived

Nellie and Ethel Noland visit the farm. *Truman Library*.

several homes down in another home on North Delaware, but she would visit her grandparents often, and she enjoyed studying Latin in the Noland home with Ethel, Nellie (Ethel's older sister) and Harry Truman. Ethel Noland remembered:

> *After the high school was built on the corner of Pleasant Street where the Palmer High School is now, Harry came by every day, and of course, Bess was in high school, and they would come here to study—both of them—because part of the Wallace family lived in the house on Delaware beyond Waldo and part of the time they lived here with the Gateses, because the Gateses were getting older and the house was large and they liked to have Mrs. Wallace live there with them. And so, they were at the Gates place a very great deal, and Bess was over here a good deal. So, when it came to Latin, my sister was very good at it and they would come over here to read their Latin.* [133]

Harry Truman never forgot those Latin lessons, and when he graduated from high school and found himself on the farm in 1906, he would come back to visit his cousins at 216 North Delaware. Bess Truman moved into 219 North Delaware permanently in 1904, after her father, David Wallace, committed suicide. She would call the residence home for the rest of her life.

The exact year is not known, but it was probably about 1910 when Ethel Noland distinctly remembered one visit her cousin made to the Noland home. Ethel told the story in the following manner:

Bess Wallace's home at 219 North Delaware in Independence, Missouri. *Truman Library*.

Mrs. Wallace was very neighborly and she loved to send things. Oh, we did back and forth, you know. She would send over a nice dessert or something, just to share it and here was a plate, Well, we hadn't taken it back and I said, "Why don't you take that plate home, it's been around here a few days."

"Well," he said, "I certainly will."

And Bess came to the door, and of course nothing could have made a bigger occasion than that, to see her again and talk to her.[134]

One can imagine Harry Truman walking down the steps of 216 North Delaware and heading toward the Wallace home, cake plate in hand. Harry was lucky because Bess answered the door.

The return of the cake plate sparked a nine-year courtship that would culminate in their marriage in 1919, after Harry Truman returned from service in World War I. The return of the cake plate also sparked the exchange of over 230 letters between Harry and Bess from 1910, the year of the first known letter, to 1917, the year Harry Truman left the farm to enlist to serve in World War I. Truman described those letters in the following manner:

The Courtship

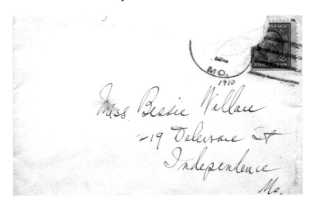

Harry Truman to Bess Wallace—the first letter. *Truman Library.*

The first page of the first "Dear Bess" letter, December 31, 1910. *Truman Library.*

Your letters are always so good and so readable that I am ashamed of my attempts. But since mine are made to get those from you I guess their purpose is accomplished. Some people you know are naturally good letter writers and some are not. I am one of the <u>knots</u>. So long as you answer them though why I am going to keep spoiling good paper.[135]

The first letters Truman sent to Bess were more formal; however, by 1917, the couple had become serious about their relationship. In the letters, Truman discussed the books they were reading, the shows in Kansas City he wanted to see, politics, religion and the lawsuit and described what life was like on a turn-of-the-twentieth-century Missouri farm.

On religion, he wrote:

> *I also have strayed from the Presbyterian fold, though I remember my Sunday school days very well. I am by religion like everything else. I think there is more in acting than in talking. I had an uncle who said when one of his neighbors got religion strong on Sunday, he was going to lock his smokehouse on Monday. I think he was right from the little I have observed.*
>
> *I like to play cards and dance as far as I know how and go to shows and do all the things they said I shouldn't, but I don't feel badly about it. I go when I feel like it and the* good *church members are glad to hear what it's like. You see I'm a member but not a strenuous one.*[136]
>
> *You know that I know nothing about Lent and such things and when I was urging you to go with us to dinner at the Baltimore I was merely thinking of giving you all a good time. That was the first "time" I was ever at an Episcopal Church and I like the service very much. But I guess I'll have to remain a Lightfoot Baptist for a while yet anyway. You know I told you that I also had strayed from the Presbyterian fold; but I went in the other direction. In place of more form we haven't any. But there are many things I do not like. For instance they do not want a person to go to shows or dance or do anything for a good time. Well I like to do all those things and play cards besides. So you see I am not very strong as a Baptist. Anyhow I don't think any church on earth will take you to heaven if you're not real anyway. I believe in people living out what they believe and talking afterwards, don't you? Well hang religion anyway; it's a dull subject, but I'll not ask you to dinner any more till after Easter Sunday. Will that be all right?*[137]

In the following letters, he described the books he was reading. He would sometimes exchange books with Bess through the Noland sisters, since the sisters were frequent visitors to the farm:

> *I have been reading* David Copperfield *and have really found out that I couldn't appreciate Dickens before. I have only read* Oliver Twist *and* Tale of Two Cities. *They didn't make much of an impression and I*

never read anything else. A neighbor sent me Dombey & Son *and* David C., *and I am glad for it has awakened a new interest. It is almost a reconciliation to having my leg broken to contemplate the amount of reading I am going to do this summer. I am getting better fast and I am afraid I'll get well so soon I won't get to read enough. Isn't that an awful thought?*[138]

My opinion of Dickens is not so rosy as it was. I read David Copperfield *with delight and not a stop. I was so pleased I started immediately on* Dombey & Son, *read a hundred pages and have read the* Manxman, *the* Pursuit of the Houseboat on the Styx, *and* Lorna Doone *and still have 500 or 600 pages of* Dombey *to read.* Oliver Twist *must have done you the same way.* Lorna Doone *is a fine story but written in such a style that it takes about 700 pages to tell what might be told in 250 with ease. I have nothing to do but read and so I waded through it. I guess I'll even get* Dombey *read before I get up for good. I stood up on one foot yesterday and this morning but was mighty glad to get back in bed. The doctor is going to bring me some crutches that last of the week and then it won't be long till I can hop around.*[139]

I certainly thank you for the book [The Mistress of Shenstone] *you sent. It is fine. I haven't quite finished it yet. I sent you a copy of* Life *by Ethel* [Noland]. *It is so good. I thought that I could not keep it all to myself. I had wrapped it for mailing when Ethel and Aunt Ella showed up. I hope you hadn't seen it.*[140]

I have found on investigation that Vivian was entirely responsible for your book going astray. He put it under the buggy seat when they started for Dodson, and Ethel and Aunt Ella had to run for a car and he never mentioned the book. He took both the book and Life *to his girl that evening and never said a word until yesterday when he brought the book home. I'll bring it myself next time. Well I hope you'll consider this worth an answer. Don't keep me waiting long or I'll die of curiosity.*[141]

In June 1911, Harry Truman was ready to take their relationship to the next level. He popped the question in a letter to Bess:

Speaking of diamonds, would you wear a solitaire on your left hand should I get it? Now that is a rather personal or pointed question provided you take it for all it means. You know, were I an Italian or a poet I would commence and use all the luscious language of two continents. I am not either but only a kind of good-for-nothing American farmer. I've always had a sneakin' notion that some day maybe I'd amount to something. I doubt it now though

Harry Truman in 1908. *Truman Library*.

Bess Wallace, circa 1901. *Truman Library*.

like everything. It is a family failing of ours to be poor financiers. I am blest that way. Still that doesn't keep me from having always thought that you were all that a girl could be possibly and impossibly. You may not have guessed it but I've been crazy about you ever since we went to Sunday School together. But I never had the nerve to think you'd even look at me. I don't think so now but I can't keep from telling you what I think of you.[142]

He closed the letter:

Say, Bessie, you'll at least let me keep up on being good friends won't you? I know I am not good enough to be anything more but you don't know how I'd like to be. Maybe you think I won't wait your answer to this in suspense. Still if you turn me down, I'll not be thoroughly disappointed for it's no more than I expect.[143]

One can imagine what Harry Truman went through while he waited on Bess's response. Days went by, and there was nothing but silence from Independence. Truman, undeterred, sent Bess another letter on July 10, 1911. He told her that he had come to the conclusion that his proposal in some way had offended her, and he begged a response when he wrote: "Won't you at least let me know you are not 'mad.'"[144]

Shortly after Truman sent this letter, Bess responded. Unfortunately, we do not have her response, but Truman did send a reply:

You know that you turned me down so easy that I am almost happy anyway. I never was fool enough to think that a girl like you could ever care for a fellow like me but I couldn't help telling you how I felt. I have always wanted you to have some fine, rich, good-looking man, but I knew that if ever I got the chance I'd tell you how I felt even if I didn't even get to say another word to you. What makes me feel real good is that you were good enough to answer me seriously and not make fun of me anyway. You know when a fellow tells a girl all his heart and she makes a joke of it I suppose it would be the awfulest feeling in the world. You see I never had any desire to say such things to anyone else. All my girl friends think I am a cheerful idiot and a confirmed old bach. They really don't know the reason nor ever will. I have been so afraid you were not going to let me be your good friend. To be even in that class is something.

You may think I'll get over it as all boys do. I guess I am something of a freak myself. I really never had any desire to make love to a girl just for the fun of it, and you have always been the reason. I have never met a girl

*in my life that you were not the first to be compared with her, to see wherein
she was lacking and she always was.*

*Please don't think I am talking nonsense or bosh, for if ever I told the
truth I am telling now and I'll never tell such things to anyone else or
bother you with them again. I have always been more idealist than practical
anyway, so I really never expected any reward for loving you. I shall always
hope though.* [145]

Truman remained committed to the pursuit of Bess, and he pulled out
all the stops in trying to make an impression on her when he informed her
in August 1911 that he was constructing a tennis court on the farm in the
maple grove.[146] Truman knew that tennis was one of her favorite sports, and
he thought that constructing the court would give her a reason to come to
Grandview. He wrote:

*Will you please send me the plan of a tennis court. I am going to try and
make one. We have a dandy place for it. Wish you could all come out in the
machine [automobile] while all these girls are here. If I get my court built
you can come out Saturday afternoons and play in the shade all the time.* [147]

By the first of September 1911, Truman informed Bess that he had
placed the finishing touches on the tennis court, and he sent her a letter that
enclosed a handwritten directional map to the farm. He wrote:

*I am enclosing you a rough map of the road. You'll notice that there are two
rock roads [that] branch off going east before you get to Grandview.*

*Remember to go south every time the rock road goes south and you can't
miss the place. Start from 47ᵗʰ and Troost and come as directed, and when
you have come eleven or twelve miles you'll come to a long maple grove on
the left of the road with a cemetery in front—and that is where you get off.*

*Wish you'd come to dinner. We'll be looking out for you so be sure
and come.* [148]

It is not entirely clear where the tennis court was located on the farm
or whether Bess ever played tennis on the court. Truman issued several
invitations for her to come to the farm, and there is some evidence that she
came; however, there is also evidence that suggests her visits were infrequent.

In October 1911, Vivian announced that he was going to marry, and
Harry told Bess a secret:

The Courtship

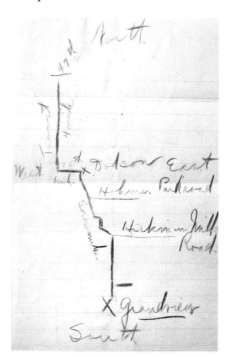

Harry Truman directs Bess to the farm.
Truman Library.

I am going to tell you a deep, dark secret. Please don't let it out until you hear it from Ethel because dear brother might manhandle me. He is going to get hooked up on the twenty-eighth. Has already rented him a farm and is going to start in business right. He sure is getting a fine girl. She has red hair. It is very dark though. W.E. can't get a thing out of Vivian without just pumping and prying, and then what we get isn't worth the trouble. But I know it's going to be the twenty-eighth. I suppose they'll tell everyone soon anyway.[149]

Bess was not present at Vivian's wedding; however, the Noland sisters were there, and they filled her in on what transpired, as did Harry. Truman said that he was scared to death, as was Vivian, but that Luella, Vivian's bride, was as calm as Grandmother Young. Bess's absence from the wedding might demonstrate where the relationship between Harry and Bess stood; however, even if Truman believed that he did not have a shot at marrying Bess, their relationship took a significant step forward in December 1911. In a December 14, 1911 letter, Truman thanked Bess for "making my Sunday invitation a standing one."[150]

Historians have written about the contentious relationship that perhaps existed between Harry Truman and his mother-in-law, Madge Gates Wallace;

however, that standing invitation Truman received in 1911 seems to go a long way in dispelling that myth. If Madge Gates Wallace was concerned that Harry Truman was not good enough to marry her daughter, he would not have been allowed to visit 219 North Delaware on a regular basis. While it is true that Bess visited the farm infrequently, it is clear from reading the letters that Harry got to see her on a regular basis, whether by visiting her in Independence or by accompanying her on the many dates the couple went on to see the shows performed in Kansas City's downtown theaters. Cousin Mary Ethel Noland agreed with this view in her oral history when, without prompting from her interviewer, she attempted to set the record straight:

> *There's one myth that I would like to nail. And that is that Mrs. Wallace didn't approve of that match. Had you ever heard that?*
>
> *Oh, it couldn't be more erroneous. It just couldn't be. She* [Madge Gates Wallace] *liked him; she always liked him, and she favored the match from the very start. In fact, we weren't sure whether she liked him better than Bess did or not. But she approved of him, because she knew that he had qualities that any girl could bank on in the long run.*[151]

As the new year of 1912 dawned, Harry Truman was committed to continuing his relationship with Bess. He was pleased to see the winter months come on the farm because it meant there was a little less farm work to do and he could spend more time with Bess. He told her:

> *If people at Grandview find out I pass them up to go to Independence, they'll think I'm stuck up. I'm not though because I'd pass up the whole state when I get a chance to come down there. Especially between now and February, because after that I'll have to stay at home everyday but Sunday. Maybe you'll be glad of that but I won't.*[152]

The conversation in the 1912 letters had grown more personal and was reflective of a couple who seemed to be very much in love; however, Truman's love was tempered by the fact that he wanted to provide a home and have a secure job for his future bride. In January 1912, he wrote:

> *I have something I want to say now while it's on my mind. I think you look better in that black dress you wore Thursday evening than in anything I ever saw you wear. I intended telling you so when you wore it to the show in K.C. but the proper opportunity didn't appear. The* strawberry

blonde isn't in it with you when you wear that dress. Or any other time for that matter. That sounds awful mushy don't it? It's not though when it is meant. Will you please tell me how you made that caramel dessert you had for dinner the time before this last when I was there? I can taste that from memory yet. It was undoubtedly nectar of the gods. I am going to coerce Mary into making me enough to founder on if you tell me how it's made.

He concluded the letter by telling Bess, "I may even persuade you to run off with me someday when you're not in your right mind exactly."[153]

The couple continued their banter in another letter Harry sent to Independence later in the month:

I wrote you the craziest letter after I got to K.C. Tuesday evening you would ever read. I didn't have the nerve to send it next day. Did you know you made a most excellent joke Sunday evening and neither of us laughed? I had asked you if you weren't tired of my hanging around so long at a time. You of course said I was [the one] who would get tired and I said I'd never get tired. Then you, thinking I suppose that something was coming sure enough, grabbed the weather and said, "Oh heck I wish I had some rubber boots!" And we never laughed. I'm glad, for I meant it. You shouldn't have been afraid of my getting slushy or proposing until I can urge you to come to as good a home as you have already. I don't think any man should expect a girl to go to a less comfortable home than she's used to. I'd just like to be rich for two reasons. First, to pay my debts and give Mamma a fine house to live in, and, second and greatest, I'd make love to you so hard you'd either have to say yes or knock me on the head. Still, if I thought you cared a little I'd double my efforts to amount to something and maybe would succeed. I wouldn't ask you to marry me if I didn't.[154]

The rest of 1912 was filled with more dates, trips to Independence and farm work. Spring, summer and fall were busy farm seasons, and yet Truman managed to sustain his relationship with Bess with dates, letters and visits. Those letters were usually mailed on Monday evening for a Wednesday arrival, followed by the standing Sunday visit.[155]

As the year 1913 opened, the relationship continued much like it had in 1912. In this year, the couple decided to exchange photographs. This seemed to be a big deal. When Truman learned that Bess wanted a photograph of him, he was elated:

You have succeeded in enlarging the size of my hat. The idea of anyone especially you, ever wanting to decorate my striking likeness with a silver frame has almost made me unable to contain myself with any degree of satisfaction…You may be sure I'd never have the effrontery to offer my photo to you because that, it seems to me, would be a case of rank egotism. You want one, you ask for it, you swell my head, make me feel good which is a good deed anyway…A silver frame! I can't live it down. Now don't forget I want yours worse than ever.[156]

February 13, 1913, marked Bess's twenty-eighth birthday, and Harry Truman remembered it by sending roses. A few days later, he took the photographs that he would eventually send to Bess, and he described them to her:

I busted a camera into four pieces today. I told the lady manager I wanted to get my face in a small enough space to go inside the rim of a silver dollar. I can tell you if I succeeded or not day after tomorrow. It always makes me feel embarrassed to get in front of a picture machine…This picture is going to be as small as you want it to be. It sure would be a shame to waste any good money to frame it. It will be too highly honored just by your accepting it.[157]

As for Bess's photo, she kept him waiting. He was still asking for it in 1914. Despite not having her photograph, Harry Truman vividly recalled what he thought of her appearance in a July 1913 letter. He wrote:

Did you ever see the Madonna in the moon? I imagined I saw her. The proper directions are to think of your girl's countenance and then you can see it. I don't know how the girls are supposed to see it. Probably imagine that they are gazing into a mirror. I'd rather look at the real thing than to hurt my eyes and pain my head gazing into the moon's face. Not that I'd ever have to put forth any effort whatever to conjure up your face because it's always in plain sight. I never see a pretty girl or the picture of one that I don't think, well if she didn't have this imperfection or that one why she'd look like Bess. You know perfection can only be reached once. You're it. So what's the use of imagining you in the moon when I can see yourself at Independence.[158]

Toward the end of 1913, the letters grew increasingly intense, and Truman was on the edge of asking her to marry him; however, he held back. The reason they did not marry could be found in a letter that Harry sent to Bess in October. He told her:

The Courtship

If I could only make money as easily as I can stir up a racket, I'd have begged, persuaded, or cajoled you into thinking Harry was the nicest boy in seventeen states. But never mind, my ship's going to come in yet and if it doesn't have you aboard it'll be a charred hulk and not worth the candle. You know, I told you once before that I thought you the superlative of excellence in everything and I think it harder all the time. I've been crazy about you ever since I can remember. I hope it's a mutual admiration society because then I can work harder and not get half so tired. You know, when the motive's strong enough a man can do anything if he's got the stuff in him. Perhaps I haven't got it but there is nothing like trying to find out.

Who knows, I may be His Excellency the Governor of Montana someday (hee haw). How would you like to be Mrs. Governor?

I dreamed that I owned a German silver mine in Wyoming last night! Wasn't that a grand dream on a piece of bride's cake?[159]

Truman's second proposal came in early November 1913, and the tone of the letter suggested that it was a success:

Your letter has made a confirmed optimist out of me sure enough. I know now that everything is good and grand and this footstool is a fine place to be. I have been all up in the air, clear above earth ever since it came. I guess you thought I didn't have much sense Sunday, but I just couldn't say anything— only just sit and look. It doesn't seem real that you should care for me. I have always hoped you should but some way feared very much you wouldn't. You know, I've always thought that the best man in the world is hardly good enough for any woman. But when it comes to the best girl in all the universe caring for an ordinary gink like me—well, you'll have to let me get used to it.

Do you want to be a farmer? Or shall I do some other business. When Mamma wins her suit and we get all the lawyers and things out of the way I will then have a chance for myself...You may be sure I'm not going to wait till I'm Montana's chief executive to ask you to be Mrs. Governor, but I sure want to have some decent place to ask you to. I'm hoping it won't be long. I wish it was tomorrow. Let's get engaged anyway to see how it feels. No one need know it but you and me until we get ready to tell it anyway. If you see a man you think more of in the meantime, engagements are easy enough broken. I've always said I'd have you or no one and that's what I mean to do.

Bess, why am I an enigma? I try to be just what I am and tell the truth about as much as the average person. If there's anything you don't understand, I'll try and explain or remedy it. I feel very much stuck up at being called one, especially by you, for I always labored under the impression that it took smart people to be one. This letter seems to me be more erratic and incoherent than the last, but you shouldn't blame me very much because I'm all puffed up and hilarious and happy and anything else that happens to a fellow when he finds his lady love thinks more of him than the rest of the beasts.[160]

Bess's approval and their quiet engagement was confirmed in his November 10, 1913 letter:

How does it feel being engaged to a clodhopper who has ambitions to be Governor of Montana and Chief Executive of U.S. He'll do well if he gets to be a retired farmer. That was sure a good dream though, and I have them in the daytime, even night, along the same line. It looks like an uphill business sometimes though. But I intend to keep peggin' away and I suppose I'll arrive at something. You'll never be sorry if you take me for better or for worse because I'll always try to make it better.[161]

The farmer from Grandview continued to be elated about his engagement. He wrote:

I know your last letter word for word and then I read it some forty times a day. Oh please send me another like it. I wear it in my left breast pocket. I'm going to put it in a safety vault to keep from wearing it out. You really didn't know I had so much softness and sentimentality in me did you? I'm full of it. But I'd die if I had to talk it. I can tell you on paper how much I love you and what one grand woman I think you, but to tell it to you I can't. I'm always afraid I'd do it so clumsily you'd laugh. Then I'd die really. When a person's airing his most sacred thoughts he's very easily distressed. No one ever knew I ever had any but you. You are the one girl I'd ever want to tell them to. I could die happy doing something for you...Since I can't rescue you from any monster or carry you from a burning building or save you from a sinking ship—simply because I'd be afraid of the monsters, couldn't carry you, and can't swim— I'll have to go to work and make money enough to pay my debts and then get you to take me for what I am: just a common everyday man whose instincts are to be ornery, who's anxious to be right. You'll not have any trouble getting along with me for I'm awful good-natured, and I'm sure we'd live happy ever after sure enough. I'm writing this at 1:00 A.M. just because I can't help it and if you get tired of it, as Agnes' beau said, put it in the kitchen stove...Do you suppose your mother'll care for me well enough to have me in her family?[162]

The Courtship

Truman had to have been elated at her quick response; however, the informal engagement would remain in force for the next three years. When Bess asked him to get married before he shipped out for service in World War I, Harry refused this time, telling her he would rather her not become engaged to a prospective cripple. The farmer from Grandview struggled to end the lawsuit, and he really thought long and hard about continuing on as a farmer. He seemed to think he could do better than farming, and yet Bess seemed content with his station in life and was very supportive of her beau. Heading into 1914, Truman would need her support more than ever, and the relationship would continue to grow and develop, fostered in part by Truman's acquisition of an automobile that drastically cut down the time it took to travel from Grandview to Independence and back.

Truman's quest for an automobile began in 1912, but the unsettled lawsuit prevented him from obtaining one. In January 1914, he renewed his pursuit for a car when he wrote to Bess:

> *You may be sure that I would never want to waste an evening in sleep that could be spent at 219 Delaware Street. That's one reason I want an auto so badly. I could do a day's work and still arrive in your town at a reasonable hour. I suppose if I did have one, I'd learn to do my sleeping between stops. There's no doubt that it would not be worn out standing still.*[163]

In April 1914, Harry Truman acquired the automobile he had longed for. The automobile was important to the Truman family and to his courtship with Bess. Mary Jane learned to drive the Stafford, and Truman literally drove the wheels off the vehicle by driving most of the roads in Jackson County. He told Bess, "Roads in Jackson County are becoming as familiar to me as the two blocks from Union to Delaware formerly were, and that's a fair acquaintance."[164] He would sometimes pick up Bess, along with her brothers, Frank and George, and their dates, and go on fishing excursions on the Little Blue or on picnics in the Jackson County countryside.

Truman seemed to have turned a personal corner with the acquisition of the Stafford in April; however, in August 1914, his father fell ill. Truman had to focus on the farm and his family, and Bess focused on and encouraged him during this time. He shared his thoughts about the situation with her:

> *I can't write you a good letter, Bess, this evening. I am somewhat worried and continually thinking of what I'll do without my pappy. It doesn't seem at all possible to get on without him. It sure was nice of you to call up,*

Mutual friends of Harry Truman and Bess Wallace, taken in 1916 at her house. *Left to right*: Alden Millard, Caroline Southern, Truman, May Wallace and George Wallace (Bess's brother). *Truman Library*.

and as usual I couldn't think of anything to say over the phone. I guess I can't get in this week. I have to take Papa to town tomorrow and next day and run the farm. But remember I want to come over and sure would if I could.[165]

Bess demonstrated her support by sending him letters of encouragement during this time, and Truman acknowledged their impact when he wrote:

Your good letters sure help to put that backbone into me to accomplish what I've set out to do in spite of the devil and all his angels. That's some job too. When the finest girl in all the world has faith in a fellow's ability to win he's simply got to do it, that's all. You know sometimes things do look awful discouraging and just one little word of encouragement will clear the whole horizon. I guess I'm rather simple anyway to have expected to get the world by the tail in five years on a big farm. It never even occurred to me that crop failures ever came here and as for operations and doctor bills and lawyer fees—well, they were never even remotely possible to me five years ago. Well, as you know, the whole bunch has happened in one year and in almost every year at least one of them has occurred. But, as I said before, I think I can win yet and I will, the Lord willing and you thinking so.[166]

The Courtship

In November 1914, Harry Truman's worst fear was realized: his father died. He turned to Bess for support and encouragement, and Bess was in a unique position to assist him because she had also experienced the devastating loss of a parent in 1904, when her father, David Wallace, took his own life. Truman told Bess:

> *You've no idea how much he [John A. Truman] appreciated the flowers you sent him when he was at the hospital. He wouldn't let the nurse throw them away until they were entirely gone. He was very particular to point them out to Aunt Ella and tell her where they came from. We certainly appreciated the flowers that you and your mother and Frank and George sent to the funeral. Your good letter also helped out wonderfully. I can't tell you how much good it really did me.[167]*

Bess attended the funeral, which was held at the Truman farm. Ethel Noland remembered:

> *When Uncle John died Bess went with us to the funeral. The funeral service was conducted at the home in Grandview and then he was buried in Forest Hill Cemetery. And she went on the train as I was telling you, on the streetcar to Sheffield and then we took the Frisco and went on that to Grandview.[168]*

It could be argued that the death of John A. Truman was a liberating experience for Harry. After all, he was the Truman in the Truman & Son farming venture that the two formed after Vivian married and left the farm in 1911. His father was demanding and, as Harry told Bess, was always the one that made the farm go. Truman had to make a choice: stay with farming or look for other options. He chose to look for other options; however, this had to have had an impact on the Truman family, especially his mother and sister. While Truman was out pursuing other options, he left his mother and sister in charge of the farm. It is unclear what they thought about their son and brother's newfound freedom, but Truman was ready to try something that might provide a significant financial reward and allow him to marry Bess Wallace. Interestingly enough, from late April until early November 1915, no letters survive that detail the courtship between Harry and Bess. It was during this time, as previously noted, that he went to Texas to try and acquire farmland, and he continued that interest in early 1916. He had made previous attempts in 1913 but did not acquire any additional land.

Shortly before his uncle Harrison Young's death, in August 1916, Truman became seriously engaged in a mining pursuit that significantly took him away from the farm, which meant that the management of the farm fell to his mother and, primarily, his sister. The farm continued to employ the use of hired hands, with whom, increasingly, Mary Jane had to work. This was Harry Truman's first real gamble, and it strained the Truman family's ability to keep the farm running. In the end, Truman would lose—something he was used to doing—but he still managed.

The question is why would Truman take such a risk at this point in his life? Part of the answer can be found in a letter he sent to Bess in 1916, when he was trying his best to be a land speculator in Texas. He wrote:

> *I am getting very impatient of my slow progress at home. You know my prospects there were of the brightest at the outset and one disaster after another has almost put me to the bad. I still have a good fighting chance to make things go on the farm if Uncle Harry will manage to live about five or six years yet. I am hoping he will. But this proposition I am looking over has a fine face on it, and if as Herndon says I can take it on and get someone to run it for me, I can make a very large stake in a short time. You know I am most anxious to do that for the most excellent reason that I am crazy to marry you. In the last year my finances have seemed to put me farther from that happy event rather than closer to it. Sometimes, in fact nearly every time I see you, I want to urge you to throw prudence to the winds and take me anyway just as things are and take a chance on my ever making good and then I think of all the debts I'm saddled with and of my present inability even to buy you a decent ring and I haven't the nerve to do it.*
>
> *I want you to keep backing me to win though and I will. When I see how happy Frank and Vivian are and how easily they seem to do it I am mad with envy. Then I see myself in an ideal country home with everything as it should be and you to run it and me and it's almost unbearable to wait. Then I wake up and see our old house going to wreck for want of paint and repairs because I must pay interest on a debt I had no hand in making and my dream has to keep waiting. Sometimes I am nearly persuading Mamma to sell the whole works for what it will bring and pay out; and then I think how she loves the old place that's been home to her so long. Then I think maybe next year will be a rousing crop and I can pay the major part of things and build me a bungalow.*[169]

The Courtship

When the land speculation did not work out, Truman took a gamble with Jerry Culbertson and Thomas R. Hughes and formed the T.C.H. Mining Company in March 1916. Hughes, like Truman, was a farmer, and he thought the mining venture would turn a quick profit. Alonzo Hamby noted that Tom Hughes, who was the former sheriff of Cass County, introduced Harry Truman to Jerry Culbertson, who at one time served as the prosecuting attorney for Cass County.[170] At the time of their meeting, it was clear that Culbertson was the most prominent of the three. He was well educated, having completed a law degree at the state university in 1896. In 1900, he was elected prosecuting attorney for Cass County on the Democratic ticket. He moved to Kansas City in 1905 and became involved in mining and land business. Culbertson's role in the company was one of promotion—trying to get people to buy shares in the company—while Harry Truman and Thomas Hughes were to be the on-site managers of the mine.[171]

The mining venture took Truman away from the farm and from Bess. The standing Sunday invitation would be hard to accept because Commerce, Oklahoma, was about 150 miles away from Bess's home. If he couldn't arrive on Sunday, perhaps his letters could, and despite this gamble, his mother and Bess supported his decision to try and strike it rich. His letters were usually upbeat and positive, and his objective was clear, as he revealed in the following letter:

> *I suppose you are tired of learning of the mine and how much I'm going to make but I've just got to tell someone about it and you're the only one I care to tell. I even tell Jerry Culbertson that I expect to lose all I've put into the blamed thing but I don't expect to   not by a jug full. If the bloomin' thing fails to connect I'll be so disappointed I won't know straight up from crossways. Jerry says the "hinges of destiny" are greased for our door of opportunity to open. Jerry has oratorical ambitions I think.*
>
> *I'll take a shot at something else if this loses (I have a loose head) and win anyway. You know I've got to win. Hold the thought. I'm going to have the best farm in Jackson County and one in the Pecos Valley for winter with a Pierce Arrow to ride in—and be a rube.[172]*

Interestingly, Truman kept the books for his new venture, as he had the farm accounts, and was also responsible for hiring all the positions required to run the mine. He told Bess:

> *I have gotten real penurious and am now staying at the plant nights. Last night was the first night. I tried to hire a watchman and he wanted $2.50 a*

night just to sleep here. I was paying fifty cents a night for someplace to sleep so I bought me a cot and mattress for $4.50 and now I consider that I'm making $3.00 a night by sleeping in a better place than I was paying fifty cents for. I expected all sorts of haunts and things to bother me, but if they came around I never saw them…Jerry wanted me to give him a thirty-day option on my share for $10,000 but I didn't. [173]

The optimism that Truman displayed in April was waning by May. He described the situation to Bess:

The mine has gone by the board. I have lost out on it entirely. If Uncle Harry had not been sick I should have gone down there Tuesday evening. It is a setback from which I don't suppose I shall very soon recover. If I don't lose all the livestock I have, it will only be because I shall turn it over to Mamma. I shall join the class who can't sign checks of their own I suppose. It is a hard nut to crack but it has to be done. There was never one of our name who had sense enough to make money. I am no exception.

I shall endeavor to make the farm go as usual but I'll have to stay on it. My finances are completely exhausted and I suppose they'll remain so for some months to come. Perhaps at some future date I'll get a mine or something that will make money.

We are very uneasy about Uncle Harry. It would just be our luck for him to die now and leave everything he has in a mess. It is to be expected.

I hope you will have some patience with me and let me come down sometimes (when I have the carfare). You would do better perhaps if you pitch me into the ash heap and pick someone with more sense and ability and not such a soft head. My position seems to be that of following a mule up a corn row rather than directing the centers of finance. I hope I never send you another letter as foolish as this one but I thought I ought to tell you, and if Uncle Harry does not improve I'll have to stay with him. [174]

Uncle Harry (Harrison) Young died in August 1916, and Truman turned to his old Masonic friend Frank Blair to provide a loan for the struggling lead mine. He told Bess:

The T.C.H. mining company is on its feet again. You would never guess who did it either. Mr. James Frank Blair. I just couldn't see the thing go clean to pieces without some effort to save it. Jerry quit us cold and I was so discouraged I didn't know what to do. (As you very well know.) Jerry assigned me his right title and interest in the concern and I went to Blair with my tale of woe. He told me I deserved to lose the whole shebang. Said I deserved a bump for going in with Culbertson. He knows him well. He finally said that if Culbertson assigned me his rights until I got my money back, he'd help. I called Culbertson and he agreed. I have paid all debts today, fired the sheriff, and we go right off the reel Monday. I tied up the superintendent's bill so he can't possibly collect before October. I am hoping he won't collect at all. If he was worth anything we'd sue him and get something back. But he's not and we have to hold what we owe him to get anything. He was the whole cause of our trouble.[175]

By September 1916, the handwriting was on the wall—the mine was not going to make it. Truman wrote to Bess, "We are at the point of making good. Made five tons of lead Monday and Tuesday, but I couldn't raise another payroll on it. It is evidently best to close the thing up and take a new

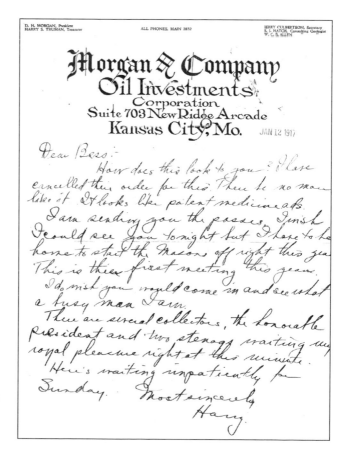

Truman's speculation in oil through Morgan Investments. *Truman Library.*

Harry and Bess
Truman's wedding day in
Independence, June 1919.
Truman Library.

start anyway."[176] However, Truman remained persistent. He returned home and promptly invested in an oil company.

It was called Morgan & Company, Oil Investments, and was managed by David Morgan, who served as company president; Jerry Culbertson, who served as secretary in charge of sales; and Truman, who served as treasurer.[177] Like the mining venture, Truman never reaped a financial windfall from this company. He even convinced Bess to purchase shares in the company, but by May 1917, he contemplated getting out of the situation. He described his failures to Bess:

> *I seem to have a grand and admirable ability for calling tails when heads come up. My luck should surely change. Sometime I should win. I have tried to stick. Worked, really did, like thunder for ten years to get that old farm in line for some big production. Have it in shape and have had a crop failure every year. Thought I'd change my luck, got a mine, and see what I did get. Tried again in the other long chance, oil. Still have high hopes*

on that, but then I'm naturally a hopeful, happy person…If I can't win straight, I'll continue to lose. I'm the luckiest guy in the world to have you to love and to know that when I've arrived at a sensible solution of these direful financial difficulties I've gotten into, that I'll have the finest, best-looking, and all the other adjectives in the superlative girl in the world to make the happiest home in the world with. Now isn't that a real heaven on earth to contemplate? I think it is and I know I'll have just that in the not far off future, unless it is necessary for me to get myself shot in this war—and then I'll still find you somewhere.[178]

As he told Bess, he decided to forsake all these speculative ventures for service in World War I. Now their engagement would be extended even further and span not just the distance between Independence and Grandview but also the distance between Independence and the battlefields in France. When he returned from World War I in 1919, he married Bess Wallace and moved into her family home. The couple would call Independence home for the rest of their lives; however, Truman would continue to visit Grandview to see his family.

6

HARRY TRUMAN: POLITICAL FARMER

I am just a farmer from Missouri who had bad luck and got kicked into a big job.[179]

In the introduction, I noted that historians have interpreted Truman's farming experience in slightly different ways. It is true that Truman's experience in World War I was formative, in that it stamped him with that important veteran's status and also provided him with another constituency he could appeal to as a politician, but I would argue that his farming experience, which included his actual work as a farmer and his off-the-farm pursuits, lay part of the groundwork for his political career.

Let's examine what he learned as a farmer. Aside from the arguments claiming that Harry Truman learned his common sense and sense of hard work on the farm—two ideas that are hard to prove—I would argue that Truman was unusual in the sense that he was the record keeper on the farm. This was noted by his neighbors in a 1945 article.[180] On the surface, this might not seem like much, but those records determined the success or failure of the farming operation. When he headed off to Commerce, Oklahoma, he also kept the financial records for the T.C.H. Mining Company. He could quickly determine whether or not the venture was profitable. Reading financial records, determining the financial success of a particular venture and collecting the poll tax as county road overseer were all activities that would serve him well as a county judge in Jackson County who was responsible for the county's budget and future road construction.

In a *Prairie Farmer* article, several hired hands talked about how meticulous Truman was in taking care of the farm equipment. One hired hand recalled how Truman instructed him to take all the buckles off the harness before oiling it so that the oil would get underneath the buckles. He seemed to pay close attention to detail, and if he took on a job, he wanted to do it the best he could. He once told Bess, "I have to drive the planter because I have a reputation for making straight rows."[181] One observer of Truman's farm work ethic concluded, "I never knew anybody who could hold a candle to him when it came to driving a planter, a wheat drill, or a binder." Paying close attention to detail is also an important attribute that he would use as county judge, as senator when he investigated the defense industry and, later, as president of the United States.

As a farmer, he seemed to be on the cutting edge of using new technology. His neighbors talked about his use of crop rotation. One neighbor observed that he was the first to use a derrick and swing for stacking hay, as well as other laborsaving devices.[182] After he left office, Truman recalled how he studied the reports of the Department of Agriculture of the United States and the reports that were published by the Colleges of Agriculture at both the University of Missouri and University of Iowa.[183] He was very much interested in progress and a firm believer in it, whether right or wrong. He did not seem to question the use of tractors, the construction of dams to provide ample water for crops or the focus on increasing the yields of various agricultural products. The theme of progress comes up over and over again in the speeches he delivered as a senator and president, and he marveled at just how much farming had changed since his stint on the farm—changes he embraced.

As president, Truman firmly believed that the American farmer had made a substantial contribution to winning World War II by feeding millions of starving people, and he believed that the federal government should invest in reclamation, public power and irrigation projects because "it gives a return of the money to the Treasury of the United States" and "creates more agricultural production."[184]

How did Harry Truman use his farming experiences in the political arena? In 1912, he told Bess about the problems in his extended family in great detail:

> *Relatives are not an understandable bunch anyway. I have always had to use the utmost tact in dealing with cousins. If ever there were any favors to bestow on one set and the others couldn't come in it has always been necessary to keep the others uninformed. There is never any danger of their telling one another for they don't agree well enough. I have been the only one that gets along with the whole works and now they seem to be using the same tactics on me as on the rest. They'll soon forget it though.*[185]

In the 1950s, almost fifty years after he held the occupation of farmer, he reflected back on the importance of his farming experience and said that the experience taught him "diplomacy" and hard work. He described the diplomatic importance in the following manner:

> *I had numerous aunts and uncles and some thirty odd cousins. These kinfolk were all on good terms with me but hardly ever with each other. It was my duty to be the family peace maker. That was also true of the neighbors. We exchanged work with them and they with each other. Naturally there were some disagreements. It was my part to help them get along.*
>
> *I also learned to get up early in the morning. In those days farmers had to make use of every daylight hour. I've never been able to break that early rising habit.*[186]

Truman made an important revelation, and given the material presented in this short volume, it makes sense. Truman spent much of his farm years in negotiation—negotiation with his relatives over his grandmother's estate, negotiation with Mary Jane and his mother over the management of the farm when he took off to be a land speculator and part owner of a mine and negotiation with his neighbors over yearly threshing activities. Truman also spent a considerable amount of time negotiating with his hired hands over their work and negotiating with the workers he had to hire for his Commerce mine, and he even had to persuade his draft animals to perform satisfactorily.

It is interesting that when he ran for his first political job as Eastern Jackson County judge, he hosted a campaign rally in Hickman Mills, which was not too far from Grandview, and asked one of his neighbors, O.V. Slaughter, to preside at the meeting. Stephen Slaughter, son of O.V. Slaughter, distinctly remembered:

> *When Harry first ran for county judge of the Eastern District in Jackson County, the part of the county outside Kansas City, Harry asked my father to arrange for, and preside at, the political rally that was held in the Hickman Mills church. That was in 1922. I was at home from college that summer to work on the farm and I remember the meeting well. Harry spoke extemporaneously and made a most effective talk. One thing he said in the talk I remember most distinctly. He was accused by his opponents of being too young and too inexperienced to be county judge. In reply he said he had lived in the county practically all his life, as had his parents, he knew the county and its problems and he was thirty-eight years old,*

Harry Truman: Political Farmer

Truman as county judge. *Truman Library*.

two years older than was required to be the president of the United States. I can still feel the impact of that statement and the excitement that went through the crowd.[187]

As county judge, Truman presided over the largest public works projects that brought roads to Jackson County, and he made a promise that every farmer in the county would be within two miles of a paved road. No doubt, he had come to the conclusion that the county needed better roads from his experience as a road overseer and from his early experience with the roads gained behind the wheel of his Stafford.[188]

When Harry Truman received political boss Tom Pendergast's support to run for the U.S. Senate in 1934, he did not hesitate. By this point in his political career, he possessed several important characteristics that made him appealing to Missouri voters. He had been a farmer, appealing to out-state Missouri, which was largely rural. He was also a World War I veteran. One observer noted that prior to his candidacy for the U.S. Senate, he had served as president of the County Judge's Association.[189] However, a couple of others mentioned the importance of the Masonic organization. Edgar Hinde, Truman's friend, noted,

He had connections with the Masonic Lodge. He was in the Grand Lodge; and, of course, he had those Masons scattered all over the state that belonged to the Grand Lodge or the Masonic lodges and they knew him. He was quite active in that. He had a wide acquaintance.[190]

Truman as senator. *Truman Library*.

Stanley R. Fike, another friend, noted:

> *He had been active in the Masonic work throughout the state. He had a pretty wide acquaintanceship, that helped a great deal to organize support he had. The Pendergast organization in 1934 was very strong, but Truman had some strength of his own through his friendships.*[191]

In his first term as senator, Truman did speak out in support of farm programs that would help his fellow Missouri farmers. In 1936, he delivered the following speech:

> *Agriculture since Adam was driven from the Garden of Eden, has been a basic industry. Man must eat and wear clothes, although some do contend now-a-days that we can get along without the clothes. At any rate we must eat, and no matter what sort of diet you believe is correct, it comes from the soil and the farmer produces it.*
>
> *During the war, in order to feed the men under arms, farmers were urged to produce two bushels of grain where one grew before and every piece of land that would produce anything at all was put into cultivation. The war*

suddenly ended, our foreign trade ceased due to a short sighted tariff policy and a large surplus of food stuffs and fiber accumulated in this country. Every year from 1921 to 1933 saw the farm situation going from bad to worse.

Farmers are human same as the rest of the population, and from 1916 to 1920 they over expanded. Many of them mortgaged their farms to obtain more land at high prices and to buy machinery and tractors to increase production for the emergency. When the emergency suddenly ceased those men faced financial ruin.

The depression for the farmer really began in 1921. He was completely deflated at that time and was at the bottom of the financial pit continuously until President Roosevelt came along with a concrete plan to help him out. The average farm income even in the so called prosperous years was only $812.00 per person and in 1932 it was only $434.00. That is an altogether insufficient reward for that most important group in our national make up, engaged in agriculture. It is in the public interest and public welfare demands that the financial situation of the American farmer be improved. I have been reliably informed that twelve million American families receive less than $1500.00 per year income. The whole farm group is in this low income bracket. The present Democratic Administration under the leadership of Franklin D. Roosevelt has succeeded in materially increasing the farm income in the last two years. But a National Agricultural Policy is necessary to remedy the farm situation. Such a policy was begun under the Agricultural Adjustment Administration [AAA]. When the Supreme Court decided that the AAA was not constitutional, the Soil Conservation Plan was augmented. This plan contemplates a Federal Aid program with State Agricultural Plans. It is my opinion that it will be successful because the farm income must be further increased.

There has been an evolution in farm management over the past twenty five years as well as in other lines of industry. Farmers are using trucks and tractors to do their work and this has tended to increase the surplus of food products.

In 1910 there were more than twenty seven million horses and mules used for various purposes on farms and in cities. Now according to the best estimates obtainable there are only sixteen million of these animals in use. Three and one half million horses and mules were used in cities for heavy hauling in 1910. Now that work is done by trucks. Those animals ate hay and grain and helped to create a market for farm products. The farmer himself is using eight million fewer horses and mules on the farm now than he used in 1910. He uses tractors and trucks now and pays his money for gasoline and oil to do his work instead of using corn and oats which he raises. This helps to account for a large surplus of food stuffs. If we could only make the automobile and truck eat corn and oats our farm surplus problem would be solved.

The modern farmer can produce with one hand all the food necessary to feed this country and two or three more. Efforts are being made to use the products of his other hand in industry. It has been found that soy bean oil makes a good base for paint when the beans are properly processed. There are several large mills engaged in the business of processing them now. Soy beans belong to the legume family and are good for the soil. They put nitrogen into it and so raising them fits into the Administration's Conservation program. Some time or other industrial alcohol will be produced economically on the farm because the oil supply cannot last forever. A way will be found to produce a substitute for wood pulp on the farm and we can quit importing print paper.

The farmer has been the victim of the tariff policy of the Republican Party ever since the Civil War. He has been forced to buy on a closed market and sell on a world market. The present Democratic Administration is seeking to restore some of our lost foreign markets and to equalize the tariff burden for the benefit of the farmer. The processing tax was nothing more than a tariff for the benefit of the farmer. Thirty million dollars of the tariff collections are to be used every year to help make the new administration's farm plan a success. I would like to see the whole tariff revenue of three hundred million dollars used for the same purpose.

Farmers can do nothing else but support President Roosevelt and his policies in the coming election this year, because he realizes their situation and is honestly and correctly doing something to put the farmer where he belongs economically in the nation.[192]

Harry Truman was a strong supporter of Franklin D. Roosevelt's Agricultural Adjustment Act (AAA), a New Deal program, which was passed in 1933 to help stabilize farm production. Later, parts of the law were declared unconstitutional by the Supreme Court. However, back home in Missouri, Truman's fellow farmers gave the program mixed reviews. A Mr. Wyatt, one of Truman's neighbors, commented, "Oh, a lot of us got in it; I never did follow it too well. I didn't think too much of it. Some phases of it I liked, and some I didn't. I didn't go for it."[193] Politically, it is difficult to determine whether Missouri farmers supported the AAA.

On March 31, 1939, Harry Truman addressed a joint session of the Missouri legislature, talking about the significance of farming, and he, like Wyatt, gave

Harry Truman: Political Farmer

Members of the Truman family gather around the radio on November 8, 1944, to hear the election returns and to find out whether Harry Truman would become vice president. *Left to right*: J. Vivian Truman, Fred Truman (Vivian's son), Mary Jane Truman, Martha Ellen Truman (seated) and Martha Ann Swoyer (Vivian's daughter). *Truman Library*.

the AAA a mixed review. He said, "I am not convinced that the present AAA is working in the interest of the man for whom it was created."[194] The farmer's problem with overproduction, which the AAA and other programs addressed, was solved with the outbreak of World War II. When the world was at war, global agricultural production plummeted, and this situation allowed American farmers to step in and fulfill a number of critical needs.

In 1944, Harry Truman was tapped to serve as the vice-presidential candidate on Franklin Roosevelt's last presidential ticket, and he became president on April 12, 1945, when Roosevelt died. Harry Truman had to craft an end to World War II and presided over the post–World War II economy, which included agriculture. He described the farmer's contribution to the war effort in heroic terms, and he vowed that their newfound economic viability would continue after the war ended. In May 1948, he delivered a special message to Congress on agriculture. In contrast to his 1936 Senate speech, he noted how the situation for the farmer had turned around. Truman noted that three years after the end of World War II, the farmers of the United States were in an excellent economic position, and he wanted them to remain in that position. In order for that to happen, the United States government needed to maintain its flexible agricultural price supports, support a program of soil conservation, strengthen programs to ensure adequate consumption of agricultural products and support farm cooperatives and sound crop insurance.[195] One historian remarked that this speech was "the opening blow in his 1948 campaign against the

Truman meets with the "typical midwestern farmer" of 1945. *Truman Library*.

Republican Congress, as well as the beginning of a major effort to capture farm support."[196]

The year 1948 was an important election year for Harry Truman, and his advisors believed he needed to win the farm vote. He pulled out all the stops to do just that. Historians have debated whether the farmers supported Truman in the election; however, what is not debatable is that he clearly believed their vote was important. Out of any of his preceding elections, he was the biggest farmer in 1948, even though he had left the farm permanently in 1917. In June 1948, he launched a tour of fourteen states in the Midwest and West. While a good number of the speeches he gave dealt with controlling the environment through the construction of dams, irrigation projects, the development of public power and other reclamation projects, he did discuss the importance of agriculture. At a rally in Idaho Falls, Idaho, he told the crowd that gathered, "The contribution which this part of the world made to the feeding of the world during the war, and the feeding of the world after the war, is beyond compare in the history of the country."[197] Where appropriate, he also talked about his family's connection to agricultural production and the development of the West. In Pocatello, Idaho, Truman remembered that one of his grandfathers believed in raising cattle while another favored sheep. He said that "they didn't get along very well; but through my mother and father, and diplomacy of the third generation, we see that they can live together creditably."[198] At a stop in Sacramento, he told the crowd:

Harry Truman: Political Farmer

My grandfather [Solomon Young], *you know, owned the site of the city of Sacramento. You didn't know that, did you? He was a freighter from Westport, which is now part of Kansas City, Mo., to Salt Lake City and San Francisco. They made a deal one time and obtained 27 Spanish leagues of land in the Sacramento Valley on a part of that site that Sacramento City is upon, and if you look at those titles you will find his name in the titles somewhere.*

The partner of the old man went south with the assets of the freighting company, and he had to sell that ranch for $75,000 in order to pay his share of the debts. Now think of that! I probably would not have been President of the United States if the old man had kept that valley.

On June 18, Congress passed the Agricultural Act of 1948, which was known as the Hope-Aiken Act. It included one of the key provisions that Truman had asked for in his May 1948 special address to Congress; however, the fact that it did not include all of his proposals disappointed Truman. The session adjourned, and Truman went ahead and signed the bill. But he voiced his concern about what was not contained in the bill when he concluded, "In the field of agriculture, as in so many others, most of the business of the 80th Congress was left unfinished."

Almost a month later, on July 12, in the early morning hours, Harry Truman accepted his party's nomination to become president. In that speech, he announced that he was calling the Republican-led Congress back into session on July 26. The president urged the Republican-controlled Congress to pass legislation that would be helpful to the American farmer. The Congress achieved very little and did not revisit the Agricultural Act of 1948. Truman took to the campaign trail again and blasted the "Do nothing 80th Congress."[199]

Truman was joined in his efforts by Secretary of Agriculture Charles Brannan, who, in the words of historian Virgil Dean, "falsely accused the Eightieth Congress of trying to destroy the farm program."[200] On September 6, 1948, Truman launched his Whistle-Stop Campaign in Grand Rapids, Michigan, and he campaigned across the upper Midwest, in the Midwest and in the border states of the South until election day. Unlike his earlier June campaign, most of these speeches, delivered in rural areas, focused on agriculture and how the Democrats had been friends to the farmer. He avoided actively campaigning in the South because his strong stance on civil rights angered many southern Democrats.

On September 18, 1948, the whistle-stop tour pulled into Dexter, Iowa, just west of Des Moines, where Truman outlined the Democratic agricultural program at the National Plowing Match. Delivering a speech

Truman at Dexter, Iowa, on September 18, 1948, for the National Plowing Match during the 1948 Whistle-Stop Campaign. *Truman Library.*

before a crowd of eighty thousand that was also broadcast nationwide over the radio, Truman was direct and forceful, and he took his message to the farmers. He told them that during the past sixteen years, under Democratic presidential leadership, the farmers had made significant progress. He noted that interest rates on farm credit had dropped, farm mortgaged indebtedness had dropped by more than 50 percent and farm mortgage foreclosures were virtually nonexistent. Then he argued, "This Republican Congress has already stuck a pitchfork in the farmer's back."

Truman continued:

> *They* [the Republicans] *have already done their best to keep the price supports from working. Many growers have sold wheat this summer at less than the support price, because they could not find proper storage.*
>
> *When the Democratic administration had to face this problem in the past, the Government set up grain bins all over the wheat and corn belts to provide storage.*
>
> *Now the farmers need such bins again. But when the Republican Congress rewrote the charter of the Commodity Credit Corporation this year, there were certain lobbyists in Washington representing the speculative grain trade—your old friend.*
>
> *These big-business lobbyists and speculators persuaded the Congress not to provide the storage bins for the farmers. They tied the hands of the administration. They are preventing us from setting up storage bins that you will need in order to get the support price for your grain.*

Harry Truman: Political Farmer

Truman argued that the best remedy to this situation would be to

> elect a Democratic Congress and a President that will play fair with the farmer—an administration that will reinforce soil conservation, provide adequate storage facilities for grain, encourage production, and help the farmer make enough on his crop to meet the cost of living, and have something left over.

He concluded by saying:

> I'm not asking you just to vote for me. Vote for yourselves! Vote for your farms! Vote for the standard of living that you have won under a Democratic administration! Get out there on election day, and vote for your future![201]

After the address, Truman also delivered some informal remarks at the plowing match, and Herbert Plambeck, director of the National Plowing Contest, asked Truman to comment on his own ability to plow the straightest furrow. By this point, the crowd had grown to an estimated 100,000. Truman did not hesitate to answer:

> I will tell you frankly, that statement was made by a very, very prejudiced witness· that statement was made by my mother.
>
> I did have a reputation, though, of being able to sow a 160 acre wheat field without a skip place showing in it. My father used to always raise so much fuss about skip place on an oat field or a wheat field that I was very careful never to have a skip place. I accomplished it by putting a marker on the drill—it was like planting corn.
>
> I have had some other experiences that are interesting. In those days, we had what we called a gang plow, two 12-inch plows on the same frame with three wheels on it, and the locomotive power was four horses, or four mules, or three mules and a horse, or whatever you could get to pull it. It moved at a rate where it turned over a 2-foot furrow, and you could count the revolutions of the big wheel, from which you could tell how long it would take to plow an acre or to plow a field—3 or 4 days, sometimes longer.
>
> Now you can get on a tractor and plow night and day—you don't have to feed it or water it—you can get off it whenever you please, take a nap, come back and run it again. I didn't live on the farm in this age. I'm sorry I didn't. I don't want to turn the clock back. I don't want to go back to the horse and buggy age, although some of our Republican friends do.[202]

Truman continued to campaign in the rural areas along his whistle-stop route. On September 29, 1948, the train pulled into Muskogee, Oklahoma, where the president spoke in the afternoon at Spaulding Park. In his speech, he said that en route to Muskogee, the train passed "rich farming country," and he described how Democratic policies had made this "rich farming country" possible:

> *One of the big reasons for the prosperity in your county and your farms is the farm price support program. You know that much better than I do. That is why I was so deeply concerned a couple of weeks ago when, after a conference with the Republican candidate, Governor Stassen came out with an attack on the farm price program. And here is what the* Wall Street Journal *says. The* Wall Street Journal *speaks for the Republican Party and the special interests. And they called Mr. Stassen's statement an attack on the price support system, and it said further, "Mr. Stassen is in fact proposing a far-reaching reform of the farm policy, or else he doesn't make sense."*
>
> *I think he knew what he was talking about, and I think he was talking under orders.*
>
> *The hue and cry that was raised by this attack was so great that the Republican Party immediately issued statements in favor of farm price supports—in principle, they said.*
>
> *Does that mean that they are for the farm price program, or are they against it?*
>
> *I think you will find that they are against it, when you get right down to brass tacks.*[203]

The most recent examination of whether Truman's farm rhetoric swung the election to him in the close 1948 election was corroborated by Virgil Dean. Dean acknowledged that the "precise implications of the farm vote to Truman's surprising victory on November 2, 1948, are difficult to assess"; however, he noted that the "president did make significant gains in traditional Republican farm states."[204] Historian Allen J. Matusow, writing in 1966, agreed with Dean that there was a slight shift in the farm vote to Harry Truman, but he was clear that it was decisive when he concluded, "The 101 electoral votes that Truman won in the Middle West secured him the election."[205] Also, what is clear after a thorough examination of the speeches Truman made during the campaign is that he forcefully and directly appealed to the Midwestern farm vote, and if that appeal could be strengthened by reminding those potential voters that he had been a farmer, he did not hesitate to mention those credentials.

THE FARM FROM 1917 TO 1995

After Harry Truman returned home from his service in World War I, the family had a discussion about whether or not the farming operation would continue. During the war, Mary Jane and her mother ran the farm with help from Vivian and hired hands. In an oral history, Mary Jane Truman remembered:

> *Yes he went to Independence, and we had a sale then, and sold off all the farm machinery and the stock and everything. He wanted to go ahead and I told him it wouldn't be the same as it was during the war and it wouldn't have been. I'd never got the help that I did while he was gone; that was part of it.*[206]

Farming toward the end of the 1920s and into the 1930s was challenging. The prices that farmers received for their agricultural products remained low, and this had an impact on the Truman farm. In March 1938, the Trumans secured a $35,000 loan from the Jackson County capital school fund. Unfortunately, the Trumans were not able to pay back the loan, which was due on December 31, 1938. The farmhouse and 287 acres were foreclosed upon and sold at a sheriff's auction in October 1940. The sale of the property forced Martha Ellen and Mary Jane out of their home. They moved to another home in Grandview, and the farmhouse was rented out.[207]

The foreclosure of the farm became a campaign issue in Truman's 1940 Senate reelection bid. As early as 1941, Truman tried to work out a deal that would bring the farm home and surrounding acreage back to the family. That deal was completed in February 1945. Under the terms, C.F. Curry, a local realtor, submitted a bid of $43,500, which was accepted. Harry

Truman and his brother, Vivian, arranged to purchase from Curry 87 of the 287 acres for $20,000 and later, in 1946, they were able to purchase the remaining acreage. In December 1945, Harry Truman expressed his displeasure with the way the foreclosure had been handled. Specifically, he aimed his anger at Roy Roberts, publisher of the *Kansas City Star*, which had not been in favor of Truman's Senate reelection. He wrote:

> *I am enclosing you a copy of a statement made to my brother on the final wind-up of the settlement of the farm mortgage on my mother's farm, which the* Star *and old Montgomery* [Jackson County official] *took so much glee in using in the 1940 campaign.*
>
> *I thought maybe you might feel like saying something about the facts as they finally turned out since, I was accused in that campaign of robbing the School Fund and some very ugly articles appeared in the* Star *under the name of Mr. Duke Shoop and several others on the subject.*
>
> *It seems that the only person who lost in the transaction was my own mother, since the School Fund comes out with a profit of more than $6,000.00.*
>
> *Montgomery, of course, had the satisfaction of chasing the old lady out of her home at the age of 87. He ought to be exceedingly happy over that proceeding but, she took it, like the good old pioneer she is.*[208]

By the late 1940s and early 1950s, Vivian's sons, Harry A. and Gilbert Truman, were farming the old Truman farmstead. The farming operation had dramatically changed. Harry A. Truman rented the farmhouse for a time, and he now enjoyed electricity, which had come to the farm in 1929, and also indoor plumbing, which he had added during his time as a renter. The Truman brothers, unlike their father and uncle, utilized mechanized farming. They focused on dairy farming, and they built a milk barn, which was located just north of the main barn.

Harry A. and Gilbert Truman officially became farming partners in 1945, and their farming operation covered a full section, 640 acres, of land. In 1949, they had 320 acres in cultivation and 320 as permanent pasture for their 140 head of calves, heifers and Holstein cows. A small number of steers were fattened in one field, and another field had 107 head of one-hundred-pound shoats.[209]

The Truman brothers focused their attention on milk production. The milk barn, according to a newspaper article, was "as clean as a Grade A milk room should be" and was equipped with running water, a vacuum milking system, a hot water heater and a milk cooler. The milk production was maintained by thirty-three head of Holstein cows, and when the newspaper reporter asked the brothers where they learned so much about cows, Harry A. responded that it was from their father, Vivian. He commented, "He can look at a cow and that's just like putting her on a scale." Harry A. Truman's comment was very similar to his uncle Harry S Truman's comment about his own father's ability to judge livestock.[210]

Before Harry Truman left the presidency, he seriously considered locating his presidential library on some of the remaining farmland. In 1950, he instructed Neild-Somdal Associates, an architectural firm, to complete architectural drawings of a reconstructed 1867 Solomon Young farmhouse based on Harry Truman's memory. The library would have been constructed a few yards in front of the 1894 farm home, and the 1894 home would have been moved to the south and east of its present location. The 1867 reconstructed farmhouse would take the place of the 1894 farmhouse.[211]

The fact that Truman was willing to consider reconstructing Solomon Young's farmhouse was significant because throughout his long, post-

THE WHITE HOUSE
WASHINGTON
November 20, 1950

Memorandum for: Edward Neild

From: The President

The attached rough - very rough drafts show the house restoration I want to make on the farm at the same time we are building the Library and Museum we contemplate.

The location will be a few yards in front of the present house and will front west, facing the Library, which will face east.

The old house, which burned in 1893 was of wooden construction. I want to reconstruct the new one of native stone, concrete and steel, so it will be fire proof.

The first floor plan shows, in front two large rooms with a center hall. These rooms were about 18x20 and the hallway was about 12x20. So that would make the width of the front about 50 feet. There was a porch in front about 10x18 with a deck on top which we called the "portico."

The stairway went up on the left side of the hallway facing east. It went up about 15 steps to a balcony across the east end of the hall and then about four or six more steps on the right of the hall to another balcony between the two upstairs rooms. The door to the "portico" opened from the center of the top balcony. These upstairs rooms were full height in the center for half their width but sloped with roof on each side for the other half - 1/4 on each side. There were windows in the south and north ends of these rooms but none east and west. I want to put a couple of dormer windows in the west side of each of these rooms and one on the east side and have a bath and toilet over the porches on each side on the S.E. and N.E. corners of each room.

Truman's plan to rebuild Solomon Young's 1867 farmhouse, November 20, 1950. *Neild Somdal Papers, Truman Library.*

The dining room opened from the east end of the center hall. It was about 20x20 and had a fireplace on its east side. The door to the kitchen opened on the right or south side of the fireplace.

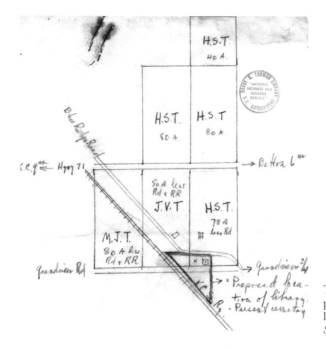

Truman's map of the proposed location of his library in Grandview. *Neild Somdal Papers, Truman Library.*

presidential life, he talked about no other reconstructions. Had the library been constructed in Grandview, the reconstructed farmhouse would have faced west, and the library would have been built directly opposite the reconstructed farmhouse, facing east. The juxtaposition of the buildings would have sent a strong message to the public about Truman's image as a farmer from Jackson County, Missouri. However, there were problems with the location of the library, and the City of Independence made Truman an offer of land he could not refuse. With the Independence offer, Truman quickly abandoned plans to reconstruct Solomon Young's farmhouse, and plans to build the library in Grandview ground to a halt.[212]

The decision to locate the presidential library in Independence freed the family to dispose of the farmland. Harry A. and Gilbert Truman still operated their dairy farm; however, the value of the farmland continued to increase due in large part to its proximity to Kansas City. In August 1955, the family made an important decision to sell a 105-acre tract of land to the Don M. Casto Company from Columbus, Ohio, which then developed the Truman Corners Shopping Center on the land. Also in August, Harry A. and Gilbert Truman announced the sale of seventy-four dairy cattle at auction, and they moved their farming operation to a 400-acre farm in Louisburg, Kansas. On October 31, 1957, Truman Corners opened to the public.[213]

In January 1958, the Trumans sold an additional 220-acre tract to B.F. Weinburg and Associates, which planned another commercial and residential project for the land. At this point, only two 20-acre tracts of land remained of the original farm, which included the home that Vivian Truman had constructed about 1930 just north and west of the 1894 farm home. The 1894 farm home also remained on one of those 20-acre tracts.

Vivian Truman literally never left the farm, although he did work outside the Truman brothers' farming operation. In 1935, he received an appointment as a field representative with the Federal Housing Administration in Kansas City, and in 1945 he was appointed assistant director. In 1948, he was promoted to district director. In 1953, he resigned his post after a Missouri Republican leader urged that he be dismissed, and in 1954 he was appointed chairman of the Jackson County board of election commissioners. He resigned from the board in May 1964 due to health reasons, and he died on July 8, 1964.[214]

Mary Jane and Mamma Truman moved after the farm foreclosure to a two-story bungalow located at 1003 High Grove Road in Grandview. In 1945, Martha Ellen Truman broke her hip, and she and Mary Jane moved into a one-story home at 604 (now 602) High Grove Road. Truman visited them frequently at these homes while he was president, and he even flew into Richards Gebaur Airport to visit when his mother was sick. That was one of the most trying times in his life. His mother died in 1947, and Mary Jane moved to 13106 Thirteenth Street in 1955 to be closer to a friend.[215]

Mary Jane continued to be active in the Grandview Baptist Church and Eastern Star throughout her lifetime. She fondly remembered her Eastern Star accomplishments in the following oral history interview:

Well, Harry and I became charter members here in Grandview in 1913. Anyway, I went in as an associate conductress. That's the first one in the elected offices. And that put me as Matron in 1917. At the end of my year, our [Eastern Star] *home was burned and we lost everything we had had. We reorganized right away and when we finally got started again, it was along in February of the following year after it burned. The year after I was out as Grand Matron, I was appointed Grand Representative to Pennsylvania, and that means I represented Pennsylvania in Missouri. In 1935 I was appointed Grand…Adah from Mrs. Wolfe in St. Louis. In that year I was elected Associate Conductress. I was installed in October 1950 as Worthy Grand Matron* [of Grand Chapter, Order of Eastern Star, in Missouri]. *So then I served as Grand Marshal for about five or six years in a row. And then I got crippled. I began to get crippled and I couldn't march.*[216]

Dedication of the Truman family plaque at the Truman Corners Shopping Center on September 12, 1957. *Left to right*: Luella Truman (Vivian's wife), Mary Jane Truman, Harry S Truman and Vivian Truman. *Truman Library*.

In September 1957, Harry, Vivian and Mary Jane attended the dedication of a plaque at Truman Corners that described the Truman family's experience with farming. While the plaque was nothing like having a presidential library or the reconstructed Solomon Young farm home to remind visitors of the importance of the Truman family's commitment to farming, the plaque dedication did reinforce the idea—probably coming from Harry Truman, who was described as the historian of the family—that the family made a significant contribution to the progress of the country.

Sadly, the trio would have only a few more years to remember their farming experiences. John Vivian Truman passed away on July 8, 1964. Harry Truman died on December 26, 1972, followed by Mary Jane Truman on November 3, 1978. However, their deaths would not mean an end to the Truman farm story.

On September 14, 1965, the director of the Truman Library and Museum, Philip C. Brooks, had a conversation with the archivist of the United States, Wayne C. Grover, about the preservation of the Truman farm. Brooks told Grover that "this was not our business" and that he would encourage the county to take ownership of the house. Grover agreed, stating that "he thought in the future the West Branch [Hoover presidential library] policy would hold," which meant that the General Services Administration would administer the libraries

The Farm from 1917 to 1995

The Truman farmhouse in 1961. The second story of the house, where Truman's bedroom was during his days on the farm, had been extended over the kitchen, and the house was beginning to show its age. *Truman Library.*

and the National Park Service would manage historic houses. Three days later, on September 17, Brooks met with Clarence McGill, who represented the estate of J.V. Truman and two of his sons, Harry A. and Gilbert Truman, and Judge Floyd Snyder of the Jackson County Court. Harry A. and Gilbert Truman owned the 1894 farmhouse, and they wanted to know if someone might purchase the house and ten acres surrounding it and preserve it for future generations.[217]

No one immediately came forward, so the Truman brothers rented out the farmhouse. A break came in 1976 when the Grandview Chamber of Commerce began a campaign to raise money to purchase the house. Its campaign fell woefully short of raising the purchase price, but it was successful in getting the farm listed on the National Register of Historic Places in 1978. In 1980, the Harry S Truman Farm Home Foundation was formed, and this organization, under the direction of Sterling Goddard, was successful in persuading Jackson County to purchase the farm and 5.3 acres surrounding it in 1983. The foundation then began raising money to restore the farm home back to its appearance when Harry Truman farmed there.[218]

The Truman farmhouse in the 1990s after the 1960s addition was taken off and the house was restored to what it looked like during the time Truman was a farmer there. *Photo by author.*

On May 5, 1984, the farm home, newly restored utilizing historic photographs and the skills of master carpenter George Fogelsong, opened to the public. The site was recognized as a National Historic Landmark in 1985. Unfortunately, the foundation fell on hard times, and in 1987, it asked Jackson County to assume complete control of the historic site, which the county agreed to do. In the meantime, another organization, the Friends of the Truman Farm, organized to help the county give guided tours of the site. The county also began to look at alternatives for the management of the site and turned to the National Park Service.[219]

Congress authorized the acquisition of the farm home from Jackson County on March 21, 1994. On April 4, 1994, Jackson County conveyed the farm home to the United States, and Harry Truman's desire to have a reconstructed farmhouse, although not his grandfather Solomon Young's house, was fulfilled. Although only a little over five acres of the original six hundred acres remained, the story of Truman's farming experiences would be told to future generations of Americans by the National Park Service. The farm home was added to the Harry S Truman National Historic Site, which also manages the Truman home in Independence, Missouri.

Notes

Introduction

1. "Truman Farm Echo in a Center's Debut," *Kansas City Star*, September 12, 1957, 4.
2. Historians have debated the environmental consequences of mechanized farming. For one example, see Donald Worster, *Dust Bowl: The Southern Plains in the 1930s* (New York: Oxford University Press, 2004).
3. *Public Papers of the President, Harry S. Truman, 1948*, 499.
4. Stephen S. Slaughter, *History of a Missouri Farm Family: The O.V. Slaughters* (Harrison, NY: Harbor Hills Books, 1978), 72.
5. Richard S. Kirkendall, "Harry S Truman, a Missouri Farmer in the Golden Age," *Agricultural History* 48, no. 4 (October 1974): 483.
6. As quoted in ibid., 482; Robert H. Ferrell, *Harry S. Truman: His Life on the Family Farms* (Worland, WY: High Plains Publishing Company, 1991), 124.
7. Ibid., 125.
8. Ibid., 126.
9. David McCullough, *Truman* (New York: Simon and Schuster, 1992), 101.
10. Robert H. Ferrell, *Harry S. Truman: A Life* (Columbia: University of Missouri Press, 1994), 53–55.
11. Alonzo L. Hamby, *A Life of Harry S. Truman: Man of the People* (New York: Oxford University Press, 1995), 27, 30.
12. Gail E.H. Evans-Hatch and D. Michael Evans-Hatch, *Farm Roots and Family Ties: Historic Resource Study, The Harry S Truman Grandview Farm, the Wallace houses, and the Noland House in Independence* (Silverton, OR: Evans-Hatch & Associates, 2001), 74.

Chapter I

13. Oral History, Mary Ethel Noland, Truman Library, Independence, MO, 52–53 (hereafter cited as OH).

14. Productions of Agriculture in Washington Township in the County of Jackson, State of Missouri for 1880.

15. Grandview Historical Society, *History of Grandview, Missouri 1844–1994* (Marceline, MO: Walsworth Publishing Company, 1995), 124.

16. Harry S. Truman, *Year of Decisions*, vol. 1 (Garden City, NY: Doubleday & Company, 1955), 115.

17. Robert H. Ferrell, ed., *The Autobiography of Harry S. Truman* (Boulder: Colorado Associated University Press, 1980), 6.

18. Ibid.

19. Ibid., 8.

20. OH, Mary Jane Truman, 24

21. For more on the corn-belt agriculture, see Jeremy Neely, *The Border Between Them: Violence and Reconciliation on the Kansas-Missouri Line* (Columbia: University of Missouri Press, 2007).

22. *Belton Herald*, November 16, 1894.

23. Kirkendall, "Harry S. Truman," 473.

24. Autobiographical Sketch, PSF Biographical File, Box 252, Truman Library.

25. Ibid.

26. Ibid.

27. Harry S. Truman's Personal Notes, Desk File, Box 883, PPP, Truman Library.

CHAPTER 2

28. Papers of Harry S Truman Pertaining to Family, Business, and Personal Affairs, February 24, 1913 [postmark] (hereafter cited as Truman Papers).

29. Ibid., January 26, 1911 [misdated].

30. Ibid., January 8, 1914 [postmark].

31. Ibid., May 21, 1912 [postmark].

32. Ibid., April 17, 1911. For the size of the main barn, see "History Burns with an Old Barn," *Kansas City Times*, November 1, 1966.

33. "History Burns."

34. OH, Fred Truman.

35. Harry S Truman to Edward F. Neild, November 20, 1950, Neild-Somdal Associates Papers, Truman Library, Independence, MO.

36. Slaughter, *Missouri Farm Family*, 10.

37. W.Z. Hickman, *History of Jackson County, Missouri* (Topeka, KS: Historical Publishing Company, 1920), 666–67.

38. Slaughter, *Missouri Farm Family*, 162.

39. OH, Stephen S. Slaughter, 46.

40. *A Memorial and Biographical Record of Kansas City and Jackson County, Mo.* (Chicago: Lewis Publishing Company, 1896), 562–63.

41. Hickman, *History of Jackson County*, 747.

42. See Grandview Farm, Miscellaneous Records, 1890–1927 folder, Papers of Mary Jane Truman, Truman Library, Independence, MO.

CHAPTER 3

43. Truman Papers, April 24, 1911.

44. For the quote, see ibid., November 28, 1911.

45. Bill Renshaw, "President Truman, His Missouri Neighbors Tell of His Farm Years," *Prairie Farmer*, May 12, 1945.

46. Autobiographical Sketch.

47. PPP Invitations-Folder General (Massman-Rockhurst folder), Truman Library, Independence, MO. Notes for a speech Truman delivered at the Heavy Contractors Dinner.

48. Truman Papers, July 23, 1912 [postmark].

49. For biographical information on L.C. Hall, see Grandview Historical Society, *History of Grandview*, 197. Also see OH, Ruby Jane Hall, 4, 23.

50. OH, Mary Jane Truman, 50.

51. Truman Papers, July 23, 1912 [postmark].

52. Ibid., April 1, 1911; Ferrell, *Harry S Truman*, 26.

53. Truman Papers, May 32, 1911 [misdated].

54. Ibid., June 25, 1912 [postmark].

55. Ibid., May 9, 1911; Ferrell, *Harry S Truman*, 32.

56. Truman Papers, May 32, 1911 [misdated].

57. Ibid., September 15, 1911; Ferrell, *Harry S Truman*, 46.

58. Renshaw, "Presidential Farmer."

59. Truman Papers, April 1, 1912

60. Ibid., September 10, 1912 [postmark].

61. Robert H. Ferrell, ed., *Dear Bess: The Letters from Harry to Bess Truman, 1910–1959*, (New York: W.W. Norton & Company, 1983), 99.

62. Truman Papers, December 9, 1913.

63. Ibid., December 15, 1913.

64. Harry S. Truman to Philip B. Perlman, December 22, 1951, 1951 Christmas Data (folder), PSF Gifts and Greetings File, Truman Papers, Truman Library, Independence, MO.

65. Wayne C. Neely, "President Harry S. Truman Shorthorn Breeder," *Shorthorn Country* 2, no. 7 (July 1975): 36–38.

66. Truman Papers, March 12, 1912.

67. Ibid., June 25, 1912 [postmark].

68. Ibid., February 11, 1913 [postmark].

69. Ibid., December 30, 1913.

70. Ibid., January 13, 1914 [postmark].

71. Ibid., November 22, 1911.

72. Ibid., April 28, 1913 [postmark]; Renshaw, "Presidential Farmer."

73. Truman Papers, November 28, 1911.

74. Ibid., February 19, 1912, 74.

75. Ibid., May 19, 1913 [postmark].

76. Ibid., November 29, 1913 [postmark].

77. Ibid., March 24, 1914 [postmark].

78. Ibid., April 18, 1914 [postmark].

79. Ibid., May 5, 1914 [postmark].

80. Ibid., September 17, 1914 [postmark].

81. OH, Mary Ethel Noland.

82. Truman Papers, November 1914 [postmark, 2 of 3].

83. Ibid., May 12, 1912.

84. Ibid., December 21, 1911.

85. Ibid., February 27, 1912.

86. Ibid., March 26, 1913.

87. Ibid., November 11, 1913 [postmark].

88. Ibid., May 12, 1914 [postmark].

89. Ferrell, *Dear Bess*, 169.

Chapter 4

90. Truman Papers, September 2, 1913 [postmark].

91. Ibid., May 17, 1911.

92. Ferrell, *Harry S Truman*, 32. See also OH, Mary Ethel Noland, 23.

93. Harry S. Truman to Frank P. Briggs, December 13, 1939, Masonic: 1939-Jul-December folder, Papers of Harry S. Truman, Senatorial and Vice Presidential, Truman Library, Independence, MO (hereafter cited as Presidential Papers).

94. Truman Papers, June 16, 1911.

95. Ibid., June 22, 1911.

96. Ibid., July 29, 1911.

97. Harry S. Truman to A. J. Bielby, April 19, 1940, Masonic April 1940 folder, Presidential Papers.

98. Allen E. Roberts, *Brother Truman: The Masonic Life and Philosophy of Harry S. Truman* (Highland Springs, VA: Anchor Communications, 1985), 224.

99. Ferrell, *Dear Bess*, 158.

100. Ibid., 39. I'm left to wonder how Freemasonry might have influenced Truman's views on civil rights. For more on Truman's civil rights achievements, see Michael R. Gardner, *Harry Truman and Civil Rights: Moral Courage and Political Risks* (Urbana: Southern Illinois University Press, 2003). For a different view, see Carol Anderson, *Eyes Off the Prize: The United Nations and the African American Struggle for Human Rights, 1944–1955* (New York: Cambridge University Press, 2003).

101. Truman Papers, December 14, 1911.

102. Ibid., January 25, 1912.

103. Ibid., October 1, 1911.

104. Ibid., January 30, 1912.

105. Ibid., December 2, 1914 [postmark].

106. Ibid., September 17, 1912 [postmark].

107. Ibid., October 7, 1911.

108. Ibid., October 16, 1911.

109. Ibid., September 30, 1913 [postmark]; May 12, 1914 [postmark].

110. Ibid., February 16, 1916 [postmark].

111. Vera Busiek Schuttler, *History of the Missouri Farm Bureau* (Jefferson City: Missouri Farm Bureau Federation, 1948), 6–10.

112. Truman Papers, November 4, 1913, [postmark].

113. Ibid., April 1914, [postmark, 1 of 2].

114. Ibid., November 4, 1913, [postmark].

115. Ibid., January 13, 1914 [postmark].

116. Ibid., January 20, 1914 [postmark].

117. *Modern Woodman* 62, no. 7 (July 1945).

118. Truman Papers, January 20, 1914 [postmark].

119. Ibid., January 27, 1914 [postmark].

120. Ibid., March 24, 1914 [postmark].

121. For the color of the Stafford, see memo of the conversation with Mary Jane Truman, May 25, 1973, Mary Jane Truman Vertical File, Truman Library, Independence, MO. For Truman's description of the Stafford, see, as quoted in Ferrell, *Dear Bess*, 162, Harry Truman to Floyd Clymer, 1953.

122. Truman Papers, July 1914 [postmark, 2 of 2].

123. Ibid., May 12, 1914, [postmark].

124. Ibid., August 6, 1912.

125. Ibid., February 4, 1913 [postmark].

126. Ferrell, *Dear Bess*, 132.

127. Truman Papers, July 18, 1912 [postmark]; October 8, 1912 [postmark].

128. See Ferrell, *Harry S. Truman*, 70.

129. Truman Papers, August 31, 1914.

130. Ferrell, *Harry S. Truman*, 70–71.

131. Ibid., 72.

CHAPTER 5

132. Truman Papers, September 2, 1913 [postmark].

133. OH, Ethel Noland, 70.

134. Ibid., 104.

135. Truman Papers, circa August 1913 [no date, no postmark, 2 of 2].

136. Ibid., February 7, 1911.

137. Ibid., March 19, 1911.

138. Ibid., May 3, 1911.

139. Ibid., May 9, 1911.

140. Ibid., May 17, 1911.

141. Ibid., May 32, 1911 [misdated].

142. Ibid., June 22, 1911.

143. Ibid.

144. Ibid., July 10, 1911.

145. Ibid., July 12, 1911.

146. Ibid., April 22, 1912.

147. Ibid., August 14, 1911.

148. Ibid., September 2, 1911.

149. Ibid., October 7, 1911.

150. For Vivian's wedding, see ibid., November 1, 1911, and for the standing Sunday invitation, see ibid., December 14, 1911.

151. OH, Mary Ethel Noland, 103–04.

152. Truman Papers, January 3, 1912.

153. Ibid., January 12, 1912.

154. Ibid., January 25, 1912.

155. For the Wednesday letter, see ibid., September 5, 1912 [postmark].

156. Truman Papers, February 11, 1913 [postmark].

157. Ibid., February 18, 1913 [postmark].

158. Ibid., July 22, 1913 [postmark].

159. Ibid., October 30, 1913 [postmark].

160. Ibid., November 4, 1913 [postmark].

161. Ibid., November 11, 1913 [postmark].

162. Ibid., November 1913 [postmark, 2 of 2].

163. Ibid., January 27, 1914 [postmark].

164. Ibid., July 1914 [postmark, 2 of 2].

165. Ibid., August 31, 1914.

166. Ibid., September 17, 1914 [postmark].

167. Ibid., November 1914 [postmark, 2 of 2].

168. OH, Mary Ethel Noland.

169. Truman Papers, February 1916 [postmark].

170. Hamby, *Man of the People*, 46.

171. For the biographical information on Culbertson, see Katherine Baxter, ed., *Notable Kansas Citians of 1915, 1916, 1917, 1918* (Kansas City, MO: The Independent, 1925), 213–215. For information on mining in southwest Missouri, see G.K. Renner, *Joplin: From Mining Town to Urban Center* (Northridge, CA: Windsor Publications, 1985).

172. Truman Papers, March 5, 1916 [postmark].

173. Ibid., circa March 1916 [no date, no postmark, 2 of 3].

174. Ibid., May 1919, 1916 [postmark].

175. Ibid., May 26, 1916.

176. Ibid., September 7, 1916.

177. Hamby, *Man of the People*, 52.

178. Truman Papers, May 28, 1917 [postmark].

Chapter 6

179. *Public Papers*, 1950, 113.

180. See Renshaw, "President Truman."

181. Truman Papers, May 8, 1912.

182. Ibid.

183. *American Weekly*, Name file, Truman Post-Presidential Papers, Truman Library, Independence, MO.

184. *Public Papers 1948*, 353.

185. Truman Papers, August 6, 1912.

186. *American Weekly*.

187. OH, Stephen S. Slaughter, 113.

188. See Hamby, *Man of the People*, 151.

189. OH, Stanley R. Fike, 7.

190. OH, Edgar Hinde, 94.

191. OH, Stanley R. Fike, 7.

192. Draft Speech File, Folder: April 26, 1936 Farm Finances (NBC) Washington, DC, Senate Papers, Truman Library, Independence, MO.

193. OH, Mr. Wyatt, 42.

194. Quoted in "From Plowboy to President," *Breeder's Gazette*, n.d.

195. *Public Papers, 1948*, 257–58.

196. Virgil W. Dean, *An Opportunity Lost: The Truman Administration and the Farm Policy Debate* (Columbia: University of Missouri Press, 2006), 89.

197. *Public Papers, 1948*, 302.

198. Ibid., 300.

199. For more on this, see Dean, *Opportunity Lost*, 92–97.

200. Ibid., 99.

201. *Public Papers, 1948*, 503–08.

202. Ibid., 498–99.

203. Ibid., 623–25.

204. Dean, *Opportunity Lost*, 108.

205. See Allen J. Matusow, *Farm Policies & Politics in the Truman Years* (New York: Athenaeum, 1970), 185.

CHAPTER 7

206. OH, Mary Jane Truman, 10.

207. "Truman Farm Is Sold," February 5, 1945, Grandview Farm vertical file, Truman Library, Independence, MO.

208. Harry S Truman to Roy Roberts, December 12, 1945, Grandview Farm vertical file.

209. "The Truman Brothers of Grandview Lifelong Partners," *Jackson County Democrat*, April 14, 1950.

210. Ibid.

211. Harry S. Truman to Edward Neild, November 20, 1950, Neild-Somdal Associates Papers.

212. See Jon E. Taylor, *A President, A Church, and Trails West: Competing Histories in Independence, Missouri* (Columbia: University of Missouri Press, 2008), 90–95.

213. See *Independence Examiner*, August 24, 1955; "Trumans Sell 74 Cows," *New York Times*, August 25, 1955.

214. "J. Vivian Truman, F.H.A. Aide, Ex-President's Brother, Is Dead," *New York Times*, July 9, 1965.

215. Raymond Geselbracht, *Truman Places* (Brochure, 1995).

216. OH, Mary Jane Truman, 45–47.
217. See Philip C. Brooks's memo for the file, September 14, 1965, and September 17, 1965, Grandview Farm vertical file.
218. Hatch and Hatch, *Farm Roots and Family Ties*, 97–104.
219. Ibid., 106–07.

INDEX

A

Agricultural Act of 1948 105

B

Blair, Frank 31, 62, 69, 92
Blue Ridge Baptist Church 12
Brannan, Charles 105

C

Colton, C.A. 32
Culbertson, Jerry 91

F

Ferrell, Robert 6

H

Hall, L.C. 42
Hamby, Alonzo 7

K

Kirkendall, Richard 6

M

McCullough, David 7
Morgan & Company, Oil Investments 94
Morgan, David 94
Muskogee, Oklahoma 108

N

National Plowing Match 105
Neild-Somdal Associates 111

S

Slaughter, Elijah 30
Slaughter, O.V. 6
Slaughter, Stephen S. 31

T

T.C.H. Mining Company 91
Truman, Anderson Shipp 13, 20
Truman Corners Shopping Center
     dedication 5
Truman farm
  acres 18
  crop rotation 34, 35, 36, 97
  death of John A. Truman 53
  foreclosure 109
  garage 27
  granary 27
  Hampshire hogs 45
  hay barn 27
  hired hands 51
  lawsuit 54
  lawsuit settlement 55
  main barn 27
  maple grove 25

reconstruction of Solomon Young farmhouse 112
sausage making 48
shorthorn cattle 48
threshing 40, 42
Truman farmworking with draft animals 44
Truman, J.A., and Son 35
Truman Farm home preservation
  Friends of the Truman Farm 116
  Goddard, Sterling 115
  National Park Service 116
  Truman Farm Home Foundation 115
  West Branch policy 115
Truman, Harry A., and Gilbert 110, 112, 115
Truman, Harry, political farmer
  1922 election 98
  1936 Senate speech 100
  Agricultural Act of 1948 105
  belief in technology 97
  Brannan, Charles 105
  diplomacy 98
  "Do nothing 80th Congress" 105
  June 1948 election tour 104
  keeping agriculture strong after World War II 104
  Masonic role in Senate election 100
  National Plowing Contest, Dexter, Iowa 107
  record keeper 96
  significance of farm vote in 1948 108
Truman, Harry, pursuits off farm
  farmland speculator 63
  Grandview Commerical Club 66
  Grandview postmaster 70
  Hickman Mills School Board member 71
  Jackson County Farm Bureau 64
  Masons 58
  Missouri National Guard 56
  Modern Woodmen 66
  road overseer 70
  Stafford automobile 67
  Washington Township Democratic committeeman 71

Truman, John 13, 14, 18, 19, 22, 34, 36, 45, 53, 72, 89
Truman, Mary Jane 13, 17, 18, 22, 34, 42, 51, 60, 68, 69, 87, 90, 109, 113, 114, 121
  Eastern Star activities 113
Truman, Mary Jane Holmes 13
Truman, Vivian 14, 114
  1911 marriage 81
  Federal Housing Administration 113
  Jackson County Board of Election Commissioners 113
Truman-Wallace courtship
  1912 letters 82
  1913 letters 83
  Bess's support during the mining venture 91
  book exchange 77
  death of John A. Truman 89
  failed mine at Commerce 92
  first proposal 77
  Latin lessons at the Nolands 73
  marriage 95
  proposal delayed 85
  religious views 76
  second proposal (1913) 85
  Stafford automobile 87
  standing Sunday invitation 82
  tennis court 80

W

Waggoner Gates Milling Company 72
Wallace, Madge Gates 72, 81, 82
Weinburg, B.F., and Associates 113

Y

Young, Harriet 11
Young, Solomon 11, 12, 13, 14, 18, 19, 20, 27, 29, 30, 32, 105, 111, 112, 114, 116
  Young, Solomonburning of 1867 home 18

ABOUT THE AUTHOR

Jon Taylor is an assistant professor of history at the University of Central Missouri and served as historian for the Harry S Truman National Historic Site in Independence, Missouri, from 1993 to 1998. He is a member of the Organization of American Historians and the National Council on Public History and the author of *A President, A Church, and Trails West: Competing Histories in Independence, Missouri*.

Visit us at
www.historypress.net